THE
ROMAN
EMPIRE
AND THE DARK AGES

Giovanni Caselli

PETER BEDRICK BOOKS

NEW YORK

Published by Peter Bedrick Books
156 Fifth Avenue
New York, NY 10010

Library of Congress Cataloging-in-Publication Data
Caselli, Giovanni, fl. 1976
    The Roman Empire and the Dark Ages.
    Bibliography: p.
    1. Europe—Social life and customs – Juvenile literature.
2. Material culture—Europe—History——Juvenile literature. 3. City
and town life—Europe—History—Juvenile literature. 4. Europe—
Industries—History—Juvenile literature. 5. Civilization, Ancient—
Juvenile literature. 6. Civilization, Medieval—Juvenile literature.
7. Rome—Civilization—Juvenile literature.
I. Title.
GT110.C33   1985   940.1   84-6480

ISBN 0-911745-58-0
ISBN 0-87226-563-3 (pbk.)

Printed in Hong Kong by Wing King Tong Ltd.

The author would like to thank all those who have helped him in
the preparation of this book, in particular Jacqueline Morley, and
also Tim Tatton-Brown of the Canterbury Archaeological Trust,
and Professor Andrea Carandini.

First paperback printing 1998

Introduction

Marc Bloch, the great French historian, wrote, in the 1930s: 'there is nothing more disconcerting, in history books commonly made available to the public, than the silence about technological development... there are rural histories where the heroes seem to work the land with pieces of paper.' Fifty years later the balance has still to be redressed.

Because of its size and scope, this book cannot hope to do the job completely, to give a complete picture of technological development and the history of material culture; it will, however, show a little of the story. Its subject matter includes architecture, costume, personal effects, household objects, instruments, tools and machines. It is, in short, a history of people through the things that they made. The heroes of the books, however, are people; and it is important to remember that all the artefacts shown can only be understood in relation to those who made them and used them in their daily tasks.

The book makes available for the first time to students of history, of art and design, and of archaeology, a panorama of 'material culture', a wide range of the most common and important objects characteristic of different civilizations and peoples. It is the second book in a series of four and presents a display of artefacts and costumes from pre-Roman Britain to the 14th century, unconventionally making the so called 'Dark Ages' fall in the middle of the story. The reason for this is a belief that the period was neither dark nor dull in the history of cultural development. On the contrary, with the Vikings, the Byzantines and the Arabs, a remarkable cultural intercourse took place among the peoples of the Western world, and it is from this exchange of experience that the character and nature of our present civilization derives.

Contents

A Celtic farmer

'Celt' comes from the Greek word 'Keltoi'. This was later adopted by the Romans who mainly used the term 'Galli', or Gauls, to refer to people who lived north of the Alps (in Gallia, modern France).

The first signs of a Celtic culture appeared in Europe around 800 BC, at the same time as the Greeks and, in Italy, the Etruscans. The Celts originally came from central Europe and spread from there to Poland and Spain, to Britain and Ireland, and to Asia Minor (Turkey).

Farming and agriculture

The Celts lived mainly in scattered family farms like the one shown here. This drawing of the farm is based on what archaeologists have discovered in southern England. By about 300 BC farmers were growing wheat of various types, oats and barley. The main crops, however, were barley and wheat. They were sown in the autumn and ripened a little earlier than the spring-sown varieties. Crops were cut before they were fully ripe. They were dried on racks and then heated, either in clay ovens or on skins spread over hot flints. Grain was stored in pits in the ground, while seed corn was kept in wooden granaries which stood on stone supports to keep them off the ground and away from rats and mice.

Some personal and domestic items found in southern England
1 A pair of scissors.
2 Gallo-Belgic gold 'stater'. Such coins were brought to Britain by immigrants trying to flee from Caesar around 57 BC. Celtic coinage started around 300 BC.
3 Bronze safety-pin, or bow brooch, with sprung pin.
4 Simple bronze brooch.
5 Gold armlet.
6 Bone skin scraper, a common domestic item in Celtic homes.
7 Clay oil lamp.
8 Bronze needles.
9 Bone needles.
10 Black shale bangle found in the grave of a young woman.

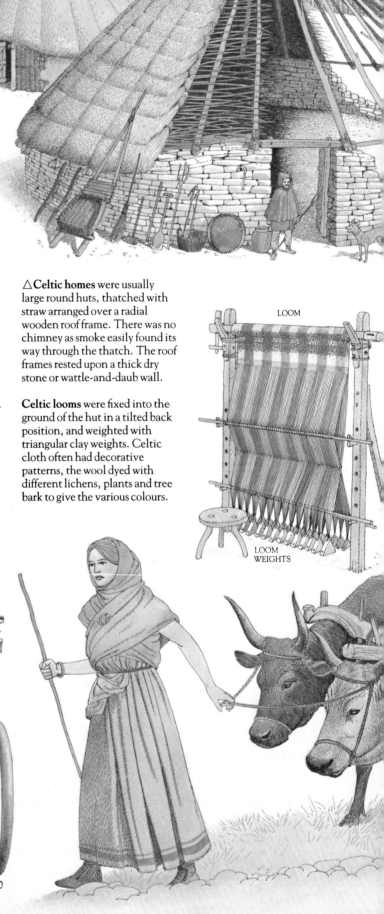

△**Celtic homes** were usually large round huts, thatched with straw arranged over a radial wooden roof frame. There was no chimney as smoke easily found its way through the thatch. The roof frames rested upon a thick dry stone or wattle-and-daub wall.

Celtic looms were fixed into the ground of the hut in a tilted back position, and weighted with triangular clay weights. Celtic cloth often had decorative patterns, the wool dyed with different lichens, plants and tree bark to give the various colours.

LOOM

LOOM WEIGHTS

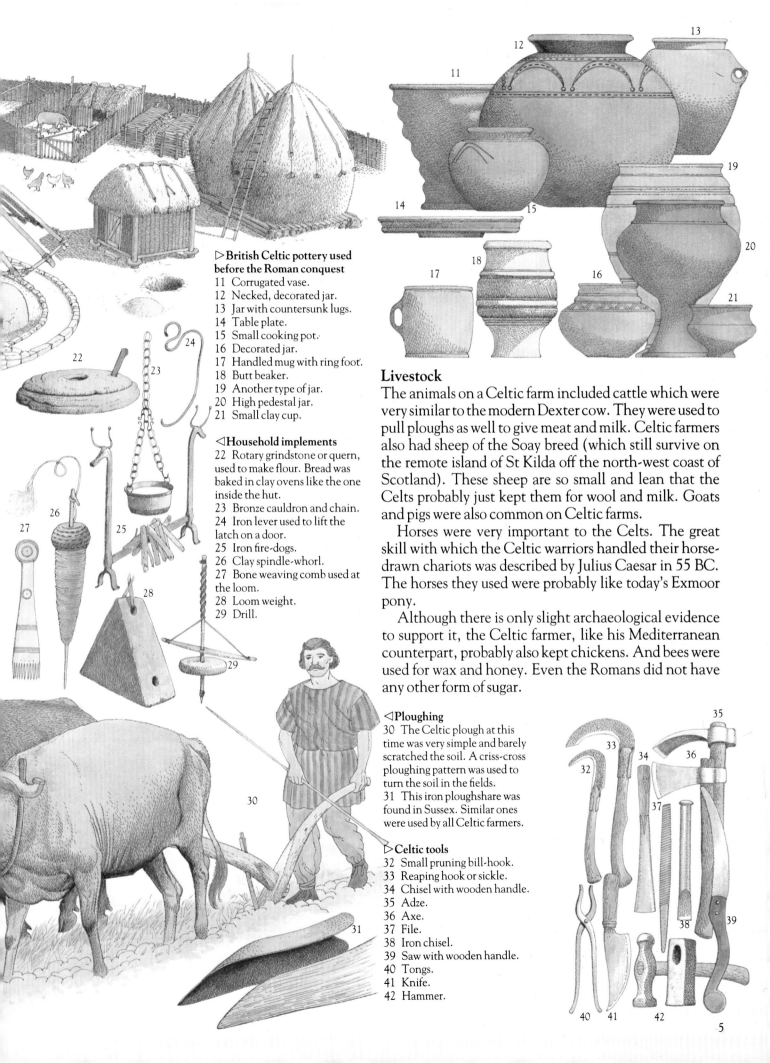

▷ **British Celtic pottery used before the Roman conquest**
11 Corrugated vase.
12 Necked, decorated jar.
13 Jar with countersunk lugs.
14 Table plate.
15 Small cooking pot.
16 Decorated jar.
17 Handled mug with ring foot.
18 Butt beaker.
19 Another type of jar.
20 High pedestal jar.
21 Small clay cup.

◁ **Household implements**
22 Rotary grindstone or quern, used to make flour. Bread was baked in clay ovens like the one inside the hut.
23 Bronze cauldron and chain.
24 Iron lever used to lift the latch on a door.
25 Iron fire-dogs.
26 Clay spindle-whorl.
27 Bone weaving comb used at the loom.
28 Loom weight.
29 Drill.

Livestock

The animals on a Celtic farm included cattle which were very similar to the modern Dexter cow. They were used to pull ploughs as well to give meat and milk. Celtic farmers also had sheep of the Soay breed (which still survive on the remote island of St Kilda off the north-west coast of Scotland). These sheep are so small and lean that the Celts probably just kept them for wool and milk. Goats and pigs were also common on Celtic farms.

Horses were very important to the Celts. The great skill with which the Celtic warriors handled their horse-drawn chariots was described by Julius Caesar in 55 BC. The horses they used were probably like today's Exmoor pony.

Although there is only slight archaeological evidence to support it, the Celtic farmer, like his Mediterranean counterpart, probably also kept chickens. And bees were used for wax and honey. Even the Romans did not have any other form of sugar.

◁ **Ploughing**
30 The Celtic plough at this time was very simple and barely scratched the soil. A criss-cross ploughing pattern was used to turn the soil in the fields.
31 This iron ploughshare was found in Sussex. Similar ones were used by all Celtic farmers.

▷ **Celtic tools**
32 Small pruning bill-hook.
33 Reaping hook or sickle.
34 Chisel with wooden handle.
35 Adze.
36 Axe.
37 File.
38 Iron chisel.
39 Saw with wooden handle.
40 Tongs.
41 Knife.
42 Hammer.

Celtic culture

The name Celt is used to describe a culture rather than a race of people, and it is a culture found over most of Europe outside the Mediterranean area. These people shared a common material tradition, art, language, and religion.

Language

The language of the Celts belongs to the same Indo-European family as Latin and Greek. Although there must have been different Celtic dialects in the past, nothing of them remains except for a few old place-names. Today Irish and Scottish Gaelic, Welsh and Breton are all that survive of the Celtic tongues.

An inventive race

Unlike the Greeks and Romans, the Celts never formed into political states or empires, and never developed writing or a historical tradition. Yet at the same time they developed arts and crafts which are among the finest of the ancient world. The Celts introduced the use of iron into northern Europe, invented chain armour, were the first to shoe horses, and also invented soap. They produced seamless iron rims for the wheels of their waggons and magnificent war chariots; and were also among the first to use ploughshares and the rotary flour-mill or quern.

△ **The greatest extent of Celtic culture** in Europe and Asia Minor before the Roman expansion. Between 800 BC and the Christian era the Celts occupied the territory shown in yellow. Celtic culture grew from the central (orange) areas, when newly introduced iron-working dramatically improved the quality of weapons and tools. This early culture is called 'Hallstatt', after an Austrian site where major discoveries were made during excavations in the 19th century.

▽ **Three examples of Celtic craftsmanship**
1 The Desborough mirror probably belonged to a woman of high position in society.
2 A torc made of a mixture of silver and gold formed into strands of twisted wires. It was worn around the neck.
3 A superb vessel, perhaps used for ritual purposes.

The Celtic warrior
4 Much Celtic tribal fighting centred around settlements, called 'oppida' by the Romans. Maiden Castle, in Dorset, shown here, could shelter 5,000 people. It was probably the capital of a Celtic tribe; its defences enclosed an area of 45 acres. Despite its seemingly impregnable earthworks, the fort fell to the Romans in AD 43.
5 Ready for battle the Celtic chieftain was an awesome sight. The Celts' love of warfare showed in objects such as this bronze shield which was found in the River Thames where it was thrown as an offering to a river god. The beautifully decorated bronze helmet was probably only ceremonial and never worn in battle; it was also found in the Thames.
6 Bronze scabbard found in the Thames at Battersea.
7 Spear with an iron point.
8 A dagger with a decorative handle and a scabbard found in the Thames at Hammersmith.
9 Another dagger found in the Thames, this time recovered at Mortlake.

Were the Celts barbarians?

In general the technology of the Celtic farmer was scarcely inferior to that of farmers in Roman Italy. All archaeological evidence and some written sources point to the fact that the Celtic farmer was probably as good as, if not better than, his Mediterranean counterpart. Although many Roman writers called the Celts 'barbarians', their farming was much more efficient than that of the Romans. As well as ploughshares, they used fertilisers, invented the balanced sickle, the scythe, the mould-board plough and a reaping machine pushed by a mule or ox. The wheels of their waggons had roller bearings – a system which was 'rediscovered' only in modern times!

Celtic contrasts

Over the whole Celtic world, arts and crafts show the same unique and distinctive styles, with very ornamental abstract, geometric and symbolic patterns. Such a highly sophisticated style and technical skill is hardly the work of barbarians. It must be said, however, that the Celts were full of contradictions. They seem to have liked fighting, often among themselves, and their religion involved human sacrifices. The disunity of the Celtic tribes and the intertribal squabbling and rivalry were probably the main cause of their eventual defeat by the Romans.

Celtic farming

10 Celtic farmers in central Europe used an implement unknown to farmers in Italy. The 'vallus', as shown on several monuments, was a reaping machine pushed along by a mule, donkey or ox driven by a man. The implement had a large comb-like blade which cut the ears of corn and gathered them into a box.

11 The scythe was another Celtic invention.

12 The wheeled plough, with a 'mouldboard' which could turn over the soil while it was driven along, was also invented by the Celts.

13 This ancient plough was found in a bog in Denmark. Although many archaeologists believe it to be a Celtic plough, there is no evidence that it was used outside Denmark.

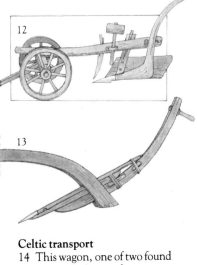

Celtic transport

14 This wagon, one of two found at Djebjerg in Denmark, was made in southern Germany by Celtic craftsmen. Used in some unknown ceremony, it has lavish bronze decorations and 14-spoke wheels.

15 The waggon had roller bearings of wooden pins in a bronze race to ease the turning of the wheel on its axle.

16 Bronze horse gear from Hood Hill, Dorset, including a terret, a strap union and a bit.

17 An iron horse-shoe of the sort devised by the Celts and still used today. This type of horse-shoe was unknown to the Romans.

18 Celtic chariots are well-known to us from the tombs of chieftains who were buried in them.

A Roman villa

Roman villas were both country residences and productive farms. They were usually owned by rich Romans who, from about 200 BC onwards, built villas in good farming regions, near trade routes and sea ports.

Settefinestre

The villa of 'Settefinestre' (seven windows) was built by the Sesti family in southern Tuscany (Etruria to the Romans), near the Roman colony of Cosa (modern Orbetello). It is still being excavated, but archaeologists have learnt much about life at this villa in the 1st century BC.

Settefinestre is typical of its period. It stands in the middle of a large estate on the western slope of a low hill, facing the Tyrrhenian Sea 4½ km away. It overlooks a fertile valley, the 'Valle Dell'oro' (Valley of Gold), where there were once several other villas.

The main building

The main building measures some 2,000 square metres. It was built of stone, bricks and mortar, with some internal walls of clay and plaster. The ground floor was partly occupied by the rock of the hill and partly by the cellars. The first floor was colonnaded on two sides and was mostly occupied by the lord's residence, which resembles the town houses found at Pompeii. It was richly decorated with floor mosaics, wall paintings and stuccoed ceilings.

The rest of the first floor consisted of the bailiff's residence, the slaves' sleeping quarters and farm buildings.

The outbuildings

Slightly apart from the main building were the utility rooms, wine and olive pressing rooms, the wine reservoir, storerooms for implements and the stables. The farmyard was also used for threshing and winnowing the corn and for storing grain and olive oil.

The Sesti family

The illustration shows what the villa would have looked like when P. Sestius was head of the family and Augustus was Emperor of Rome in the 1st century AD. P. Sestius was rich enough to own his own fleet of ships and produce his own jars and containers on the estate, marked with his family's initial and symbol. This makes it easier to assess the success of his business. Jars and amphorae with the Sesti sign have been found in Italy, France and Spain.

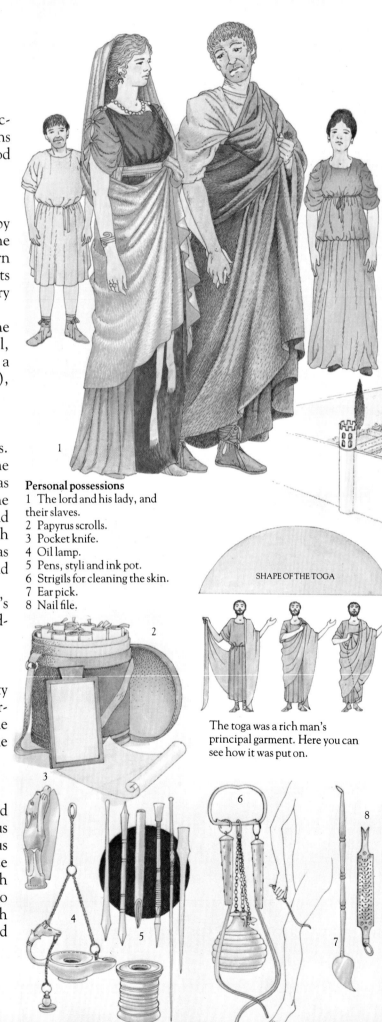

Personal possessions
1 The lord and his lady, and their slaves.
2 Papyrus scrolls.
3 Pocket knife.
4 Oil lamp.
5 Pens, styli and ink pot.
6 Strigils for cleaning the skin.
7 Ear pick.
8 Nail file.

SHAPE OF THE TOGA

The toga was a rich man's principal garment. Here you can see how it was put on.

(right) The wine produced from the vineyard at Settefinestre was mainly exported.

(far right) Map showing the position of the villa and estate at Settefinestre (shaded) in relation to other estates, roads and the port of Cosa.

▽ A reconstruction of the villa from the west. The garden walls and the arches still stand, but the rest is based on what we know of other villas.

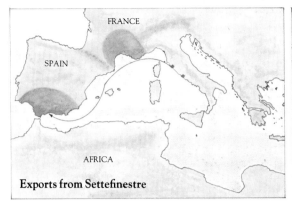

Exports from Settefinestre

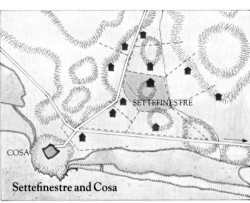

Settefinestre and Cosa

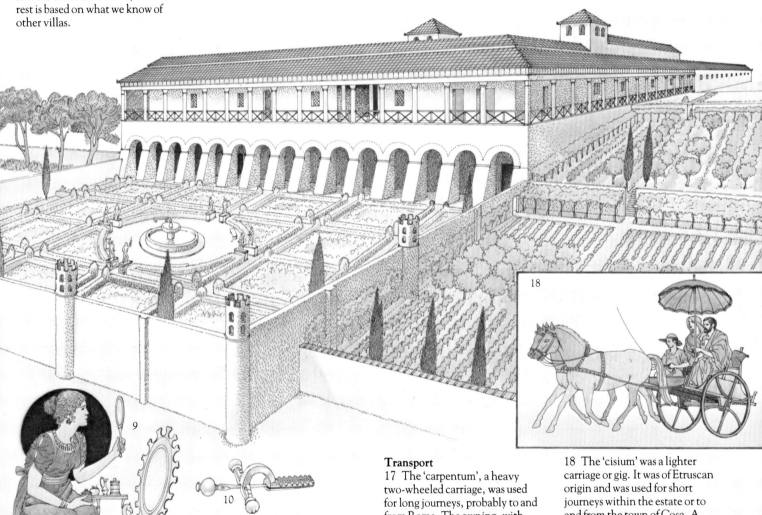

A Roman lady
9 Mirrors were made from highly polished brass.
10 A fibula used to fasten clothes.
11 Earring with two pearls.
12 Ivory comb.
13 Gold snake bracelet.
14 Gold ring with a god's head.
15 Ivory hairpins.
16 Silver flask and ivory pestle and mortar for make-up.

Transport
17 The 'carpentum', a heavy two-wheeled carriage, was used for long journeys, probably to and from Rome. The awning, with curtains at each end, helped protect the driver and passenger from the heat and dust in the summer and the rain in winter.

18 The 'cisium' was a lighter carriage or gig. It was of Etruscan origin and was used for short journeys within the estate or to and from the town of Cosa. A slave drove the lord and lady of the villa.

Eating equipment

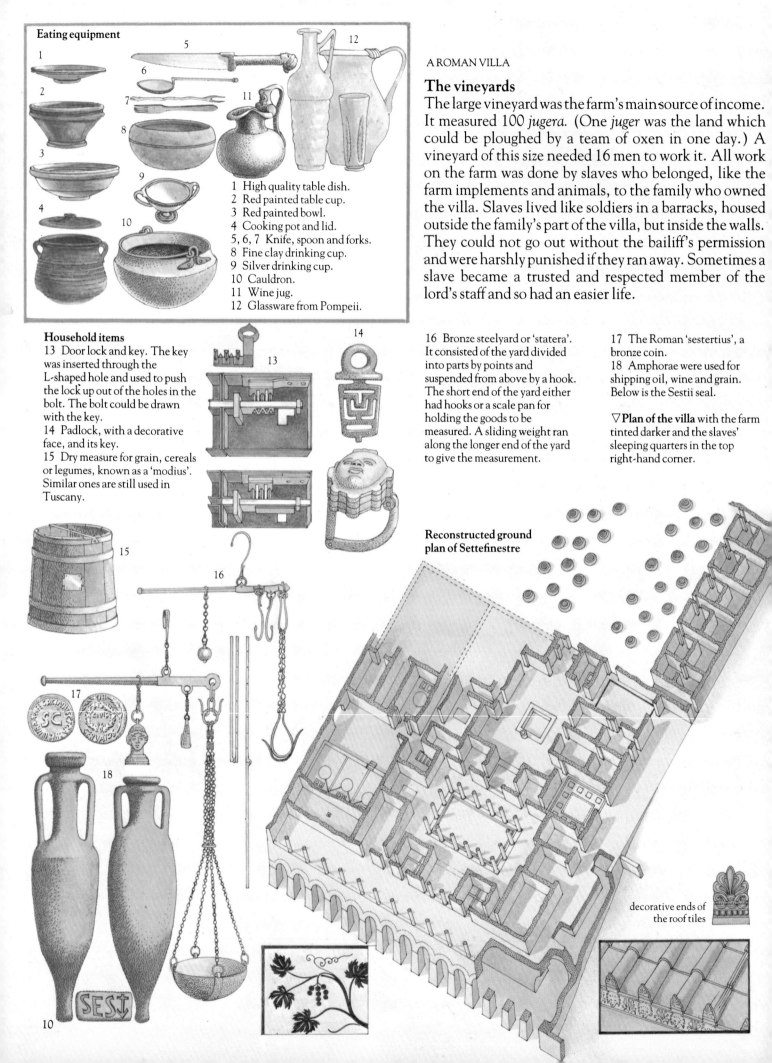

1. High quality table dish.
2. Red painted table cup.
3. Red painted bowl.
4. Cooking pot and lid.
5, 6, 7 Knife, spoon and forks.
8. Fine clay drinking cup.
9. Silver drinking cup.
10. Cauldron.
11. Wine jug.
12. Glassware from Pompeii.

Household items

13. Door lock and key. The key was inserted through the L-shaped hole and used to push the lock up out of the holes in the bolt. The bolt could be drawn with the key.
14. Padlock, with a decorative face, and its key.
15. Dry measure for grain, cereals or legumes, known as a 'modius'. Similar ones are still used in Tuscany.

16. Bronze steelyard or 'statera'. It consisted of the yard divided into parts by points and suspended from above by a hook. The short end of the yard either had hooks or a scale pan for holding the goods to be measured. A sliding weight ran along the longer end of the yard to give the measurement.

17. The Roman 'sestertius', a bronze coin.
18. Amphorae were used for shipping oil, wine and grain. Below is the Sestii seal.

▽ **Plan of the villa** with the farm tinted darker and the slaves' sleeping quarters in the top right-hand corner.

A ROMAN VILLA

The vineyards

The large vineyard was the farm's main source of income. It measured 100 *jugera*. (One *juger* was the land which could be ploughed by a team of oxen in one day.) A vineyard of this size needed 16 men to work it. All work on the farm was done by slaves who belonged, like the farm implements and animals, to the family who owned the villa. Slaves lived like soldiers in a barracks, housed outside the family's part of the villa, but inside the walls. They could not go out without the bailiff's permission and were harshly punished if they ran away. Sometimes a slave became a trusted and respected member of the lord's staff and so had an easier life.

Reconstructed ground plan of Settefinestre

decorative ends of the roof tiles

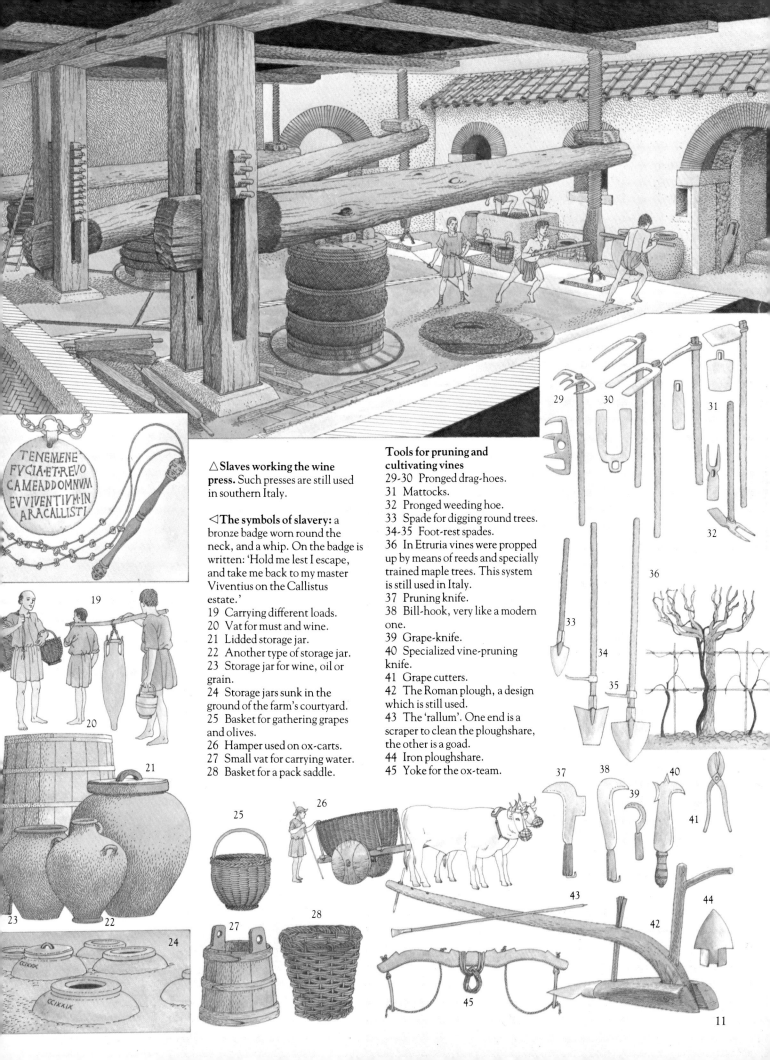

△**Slaves working the wine press.** Such presses are still used in southern Italy.

◁**The symbols of slavery:** a bronze badge worn round the neck, and a whip. On the badge is written: 'Hold me lest I escape, and take me back to my master Viventius on the Callistus estate.'

19 Carrying different loads.
20 Vat for must and wine.
21 Lidded storage jar.
22 Another type of storage jar.
23 Storage jar for wine, oil or grain.
24 Storage jars sunk in the ground of the farm's courtyard.
25 Basket for gathering grapes and olives.
26 Hamper used on ox-carts.
27 Small vat for carrying water.
28 Basket for a pack saddle.

Tools for pruning and cultivating vines
29-30 Pronged drag-hoes.
31 Mattocks.
32 Pronged weeding hoe.
33 Spade for digging round trees.
34-35 Foot-rest spades.
36 In Etruria vines were propped up by means of reeds and specially trained maple trees. This system is still used in Italy.
37 Pruning knife.
38 Bill-hook, very like a modern one.
39 Grape-knife.
40 Specialized vine-pruning knife.
41 Grape cutters.
42 The Roman plough, a design which is still used.
43 The 'rallum'. One end is a scraper to clean the ploughshare, the other is a goad.
44 Iron ploughshare.
45 Yoke for the ox-team.

TENEMENE
FVGIA·ET·REVO
CAMEADDOMNVM
EVVIVENTIVM·IN
ARACALLISTI

11

Roman town life

In the 8th century BC a group of reed huts beside the River Tiber gradually developed into a town, Rome, which became the centre of a great empire. There is little evidence left of what life was like in Rome at the height of the empire in the first century AD; but at Ostia, the port which served ancient Rome, plenty of evidence still survives.

Houses for the townspeople

The townspeople lived in solid, brick-built apartment houses of four or five storeys, set around a courtyard or garden. The flats were reached from the courtyard, or else from the street, by stairs set between the shops on the ground floor.

An apartment consisted of five or six rooms served by a corridor which overlooked the street and ended in a room larger than the rest. Walls and ceilings were often elaborately decorated.

Water, an essential amenity

To the Romans a good supply of fresh water was essential, and they built aqueducts to provide it. The nine major aqueducts of Rome had a total length of some 425 kms, with a capacity of 350,000,000 litres every 24 hours. The first aqueduct was built in the 4th century BC.

The aqueduct took water to a reservoir with settling tanks and a system of sluices and taps to control its distribution to the three main outlets: public fountains (where the ordinary citizens got their water), public baths, and the homes of wealthy citizens who paid for the privilege.

Another important aspect of the water system was the regular flushing of the street drains. By the first century AD Rome had an elaborate network of covered street drains, although it was to the Etruscans that the Romans owed their knowledge of water supply and control.

CLOTH FOR THE PALLA

Clothes worn by a wealthy Roman family
1 A child's version of the adult male dress. The ornament around his neck was worn by children of the nobility.
2 The dress and hairstyle of an older woman who wears a short-sleeved 'stola' with a 'palla' on top.
3 A long-sleeved stola.
4 The head of the family wears a white tunic under the toga worn by senators. The stool was of a kind only used by members of the senate.
5 The family's shrine; all homes had one.
6 The Greek palla and how to put it on. The Romans called it the female toga. It was fashionable at this time and the Roman stola developed from it.

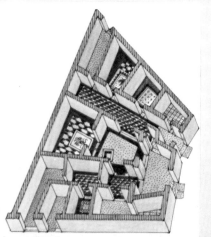

◁ **The House of the Medusa at Ostia.** The home of a very rich family, it had richly decorated mosaic floors of different designs.

▷ **The street frontage of a five-storey tenement block** built in Ostia in imperial times. On the ground floor were shops, and a staircase to the upper floors. The balcony on the first floor was reserved for better-off tenants. Below the road were the drains and pipes of the water supply.

Public baths and sanitation

Ostia at this time had 18 baths, all built to a specific plan. Some belonged to private clubs, others were public. But, whether public or private, they were the most important meeting places in the city, both for business and socially. Together with theatres and circuses, the baths were part of the civic amenities which all free citizens regarded as theirs by right.

Public lavatories were usually found in the same building as the baths, and also near fountains or other buildings with a constant supply of water. Refuse was collected by municipal slaves under the direction of the magistrate responsible for the care and maintenance of the streets.

Food stores

Warehouses for the storage of foodstuffs and other goods were another municipal service. At Ostia, Rome and other commercial centres in the empire, many were state-owned. Others, however, might be owned by private merchants or the town authorities.

Ostia's harbour

Just north of Ostia lay the harbours. Small boats sailed up the River Tiber to unload their cargoes at Rome itself, but larger merchant ships could not do this. Instead they anchored offshore and were loaded or unloaded by smaller boats acting as tenders.

In AD 42, on the orders of the Emperor Claudius, a huge imperial harbour was started. This, in turn, was superseded by a more compact and sheltered harbour built around AD 112, during the reign of the Emperor Trajan.

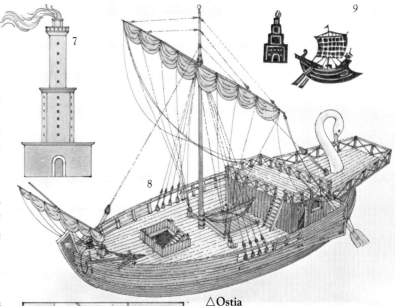

△ **Ostia**
7 Lighthouse built by Claudius.
8 Roman cargo ship, probably the commonest seen in Ostia. The ship had a lifeboat, and a deckhouse with cabins for the officers.
9 Mosaic illustrations of the lighthouse at Ostia and a cargo ship.

(above left) The position of Ostia in relation to Porto Augustus and Rome. The dotted line is the present coastline. The major roads are in red.

▽ **Tiles**
10 Most Roman buildings had roofs of flat tiles linked with ridge tiles. The flat tiles were called 'tegulae' and the ridge ones were known as 'imbrex'.
11 From the 3rd century AD the flat tiles were usually stamped with the maker's name.

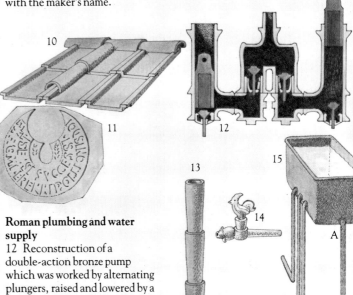

Roman plumbing and water supply

12 Reconstruction of a double-action bronze pump which was worked by alternating plungers, raised and lowered by a rocking beam. The bottom of the cylinders was connected by pipes to the reservoir.
13 Terracotta drainage pipes.
14 Bronze stopcock.
15 Water reservoir and supply: A water tank, B pipe coming from the aqueduct or main reservoir; C house supply; D supply for public fountain; E public fountain.

Bedroom furniture and some related items
1 Portable terrácotta lantern.
2 Portable bronze stove. Many homes in Ostia did not have central heating.
3 Bedroom cupboard of a type found at Pompeii.
4 Bed of the period.
5 Wooden cradle for a baby.
6 Bronze three-legged table.
7 Bronze upholstered chair after a Greek design.
8 An earthenware chamber pot.

A Roman kitchen and some of the utensils which would have been used in it
9 Set of bronze kitchen utensils found at Pompeii. They represent common designs.
10-12 Types of bronze pan.
13 Gridiron.
14 Earthenware pot with lid.
15 Bronze ladle.
16 Bronze strainer.
17 Portable heater for liquids. The heat was provided by charcoal which was packed around the utensils in the large metal container. When hot, the liquid was obtained from a tap at the side.

A Roman kitchen

(below left) The dining room of a wealthy Roman family
18 The usual arrangement of the couches in a Roman dining-room. Three couches were placed around the table and the fourth side left open for serving. Members of the family reclined on the left-hand couch and guests used the others.
19 Cup of black painted pottery.
20 Silver drinking cup.
21 Three pieces of the red painted pottery which was common in the early days of the Roman empire.

△ **The public lavatories at Ostia** were near the baths of the Forum. They had a long marble seat so that several people could use them at the same time. It was quite usual for the public lavatories to be used for meetings and business deals. Tenement blocks, baths and public buildings in Ostia, as in Rome, were all built with public lavatories. Private ones were very rare, and only the most wealthy of the town's citizens could afford that luxury.

▽ **The baths**
There were 18 baths in the urban area of Ostia and all followed the same design. They had pools heated by wood-fired boilers underneath the floors. The pools were heated to different temperatures in the different rooms. These ranged from the 'calidaria' or hot rooms, through the 'tepidaria' or warm rooms to the 'frigidaria' or rooms in which the pools were quite cold. There were also rest rooms and areas for exercise. The baths were the favourite meeting place for citizens of the Roman empire.

Tombstone scenes

Tombstone scenes

A great deal of our knowledge of the life led by the people of Ostia comes from their tombstones. Many have pictures on them showing the work or craft of the person buried in the tomb.

◁A blacksmith and his assistant at work. The anvil they are using is of a shape that is still used. Hanging from a rafter behind them are some of their different tools.

ROMAN TOWN LIFE

Shops and tradesmen

Merchants and traders settled in Ostia, so increasing its prosperity. They built luxurious houses and the clerks and others they employed settled in the apartment buildings, so forming a large middle class. Shopkeepers, innkeepers, craftsmen and small traders completed Ostia's population.

The shops usually consisted of a rectangular room with a bench near the door. The merchandise was displayed on shelves on the walls. Next to the shop was a storeroom. At the back of the shop was a staircase which led up to the mezzanine floor where the shopkeeper lived.

Between the shops were inns and snackbars and the workshops of craftsmen, such as potters and saddlers, who made their own goods and sold them directly to the public.

Slave labour

The growth of Ostia, like that of other Roman cities, was largely dependent on the vast numbers of slaves employed as unskilled labour. The great aqueducts could not have been built without them, nor would Roman cities have had their excellent water supply and drainage systems if it had not been for slave labour.

The Roman family at home

The father was very definitely head of the family in Roman times. He wielded considerable authority, including that of life and death, over all members of his family and their slaves.

The dining-room was the focal point of the family home. Men and women dined together, reclining on cushions set out on couches. Roman furniture varied from the simple and functional to the fashionable and highly ornate. Chairs and beds were usually wooden, although some metal ones have survived.

Statues were common in the homes of rich citizens, as well as in public buildings and gardens. Paintings were usually murals and generally copies of Greek paintings from the 5th and 4th centuries BC.

△Some of the many different sorts of tool and implement made and used by the people of Ostia. Many of them are very similar to tools still used today.
(inset) Man working a grindstone. He probably made many of the tools shown here.

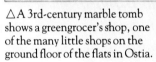

△A 3rd-century marble tomb shows a greengrocer's shop, one of the many little shops on the ground floor of the flats in Ostia.

▷A marble relief from the 2nd century shows a butcher's shop. Pieces of meat hang from hooks. Behind the butcher are his scales.

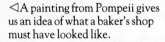

◁A painting from Pompeii gives us an idea of what a baker's shop must have looked like.

▽A Roman flour mill driven by a blindfolded horse, from another relief found in Ostia. The baker is removing loaves from the oven on a long-handled paddle-like implement.

Vindolanda: the frontier

Vindolanda was a Roman frontier fort and garrison town near the wall built by the Emperor Hadrian in the north of England. Centuries later the English called the town Chesterholm. From modern excavations, archaeologists have learnt a lot about life at Vindolanda, because an unusually large amount of organic material (leather, bone and wood) has been preserved in the ground around the site. This gives a very clear picture of Roman garrison life, in Britain and elsewhere throughout the empire.

The Romans invaded Britain in AD 43, but only occupied the southern part. It was not until AD 69 that the Roman legions led by Petilius Cerealis moved north. The conquest of Britain was effectively completed by the consul Agricola in AD 79 and 84.

Rome's most northern garrison

A timber fort was first built at Vindolanda at about this time, when the road between Carlisle and Corbridge was opened. The road served as a frontier for some 25 years, during which period the garrison stationed there must have had a hard time. Their task was to protect the traffic on the road and to maintain constant patrols on the north and south of the border. However, defence of the northernmost boundary of the Roman empire became much easier with the construction of the great wall by the Emperor Hadrian between AD 120 and 130.

Life in the garrison town

Vindolanda was one of a number of forts along the wall. Outside the west gate a village, or 'vicus' grew up, with a civilian population first consisting of families and relatives of the soldiers. In the vicus there was also a military bath-house built in AD 160 by craftsmen especially brought in from the Sixth Legion. A changing room and latrine were attached. In this bath-house, as everywhere else in the Roman empire, the troops relaxed in their off-duty hours, gambling and eating mussels and oysters. They probably ate other things as well, but excavations at Vindolanda have uncovered very large quantities of mussel and oyster shells.

An inn for travellers was the largest building in the vicus. It had guest rooms, latrine, kitchen, dining room, stoke hole, bath, brewery, servants' quarters and stables. It could accommodate a dozen officials with their servants and pack animals. There were also buildings in the vicus for the families of the troops, the 'married quarters'. Although some of the rooms had cooking facilities, most cooking was done outside on the verandahs.

Roman soldiers

Military patrols along the wall, 2nd century AD

1 Cavalry trooper wearing mail armour.

2 Legionary wearing plate armour.

3 Helmet worn by infantry in Britain and Germany.

4 Standard-bearer with the regimental standard from Vindolanda, and a centurion. In battle the legion's standard was the chief rallying point, so the standard-bearer was an important man in the legion.

5 Spearheads from the fort.

△ **Map of Hadrian's Wall** with its forts and linking roads.

▷ The main routes of the Roman invasion of Britain:

A London
B Brentford
C Richborough
D Colchester
E Silchester
F St Albans
G Maiden Castle
H Gloucester
J Caerleon
K Wroxeter
L Lincoln
M Chester
N York
P The Wall area shown above

▽ **Reconstruction of the fort of Vindolanda** and its vicus outside the main walls. The positions of the military bathhouse (A) and the inn (B) are shown.

The defences

6 Roman catapult or 'ballista'. These were usually mounted on special platforms within the walls of the fort.

7 Bolt heads from a ballista found at Vindolanda.

8 Diagrammatic plan showing the construction of the wall. The wall was 3m. wide and 4.5m. high and surmounted by crenellations. Outside the wall was a fighting ditch, 9m. by 4m. At each Roman mile there was a 'mile-castle' with a north and a south gate, and barracks for the troops. Between the mile-castles were two turrets. South of the wall was the 'vallum', a deep ditch with mounds to the north and south of it.

9 Bronze coin with the image of the Emperor Hadrian found at Vindolanda.

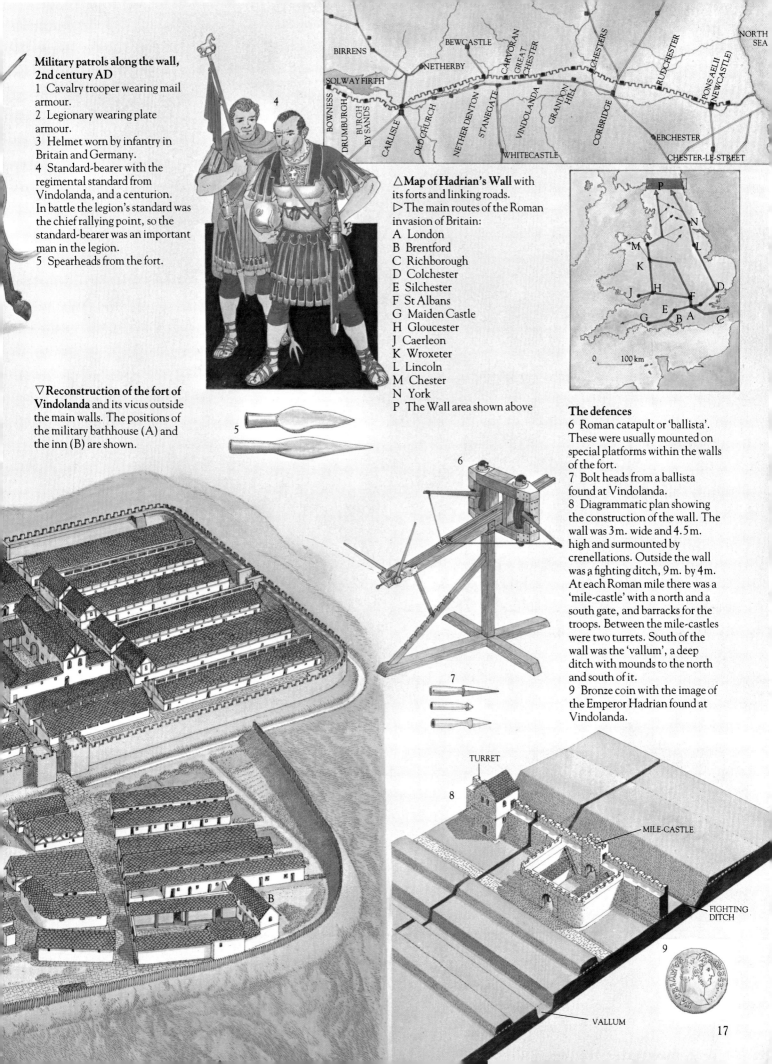

TURRET

MILE-CASTLE

FIGHTING DITCH

VALLUM

17

People of Vindolanda

From the evidence of excavations in the settlement's cemetery the community was a very young one. The average age of death for men was about 36, and for women 28. This does not take into account infant and child mortality which was extremely high. This high mortality rate was due in large part to the inhospitable climate rather than battle losses.

From the small stone altars dedicated to British gods, we learn the names of some of these early inhabitants of Vindolanda: Senilis, Longinus, Senaculus and Lupulus. Other names found as graffiti on pottery include Martinus, Gatinius and Aurelius. Apart from Flavia, Emerita and Aurelia, we know the names of few women. Although all these names sound very Roman, many were in fact just the Roman form of local names.

Religion

The religion practised by the people living in this and the other forts along the wall was Celtic rather than Roman. No temple has yet been found at Vindolanda, although temples have been excavated at other forts.

The villagers set up altars to the Roman god Vulcan, and a relief showing the god Mercury has also been found. Most of the dedications, however, are to local gods. A clay statuette which has been found of the 'Dea Nutrix' probably came with the troops from the Rhine frontier; it was not a local deity.

Home comforts

Although the people of this rather bleak frontier post lacked the sophistication found elsewhere in the empire, particularly in the towns, they nevertheless possessed most of the material comforts known to the Romans.

The houses had doors with locks, the windows were fitted with bars, and wells and water tanks provided a good clean water supply. The women ornamented themselves with beads, hairpins, bangles and rings, and used combs, tweezers, and mirrors of polished bronze. Men had bronze tunic fittings, belt attachments and enamelled buckles. Even small children wore shoes.

Official correspondence

Archaeologists have discovered 202 wooden tablets written in ink, or with a stylus, from all periods of the fort's occupation (see bottom left). One describes what military service at Vindolanda was like. There is also a list of supplies needed for the garrison. Included on it are salt, spices, pork fat, Celtic beer, goat's meat, ham, young pig and venison, as well as quantities of barley, wheat and malting corn. The soldiers guarding this northern outpost of the empire certainly did not intend to go hungry.

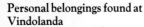

Personal belongings found at Vindolanda
1 Dress of commanding officer at time of Hadrian.
2-3 Gold rings.
4 Gilt earrings.
5 Bone hairpins.
6 Dress of commander's wife.
7 Carved gemstone.
8 Bronze cockerel amulet.
9-10 Brooches worn by men.
11 A lady's brooches.
12 Wooden combs.
13 Jet betrothal medallion, 3rd century AD.
14 Pattern of tacks on the sole of a sandal.
15 Soldier's sandal found at Vindolanda.
16 A reconstruction of 15.
17 Shoemaker's seal.
18 Lady's slipper with trade marks.
19 Civilian's shoe.
20-22 Belt buckles.
23 Infantry sword and scabbard.
24 Dagger and scabbard.
25 Details of scaled armour.
26 Multi-leaved stores list.
27 Bronze stylus and reed pen.
28 Sample of calligraphy.

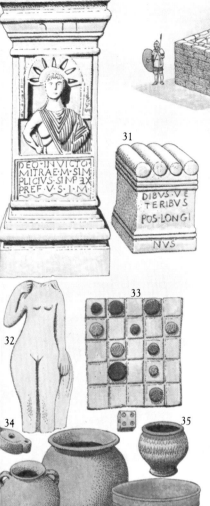

Religion

29 Altar to Mithras, a god popular with the soldiers.
30 Monumental tomb from the cemetery at Vindolanda.
31 Portable altar.
32 Headless statuette of Venus.
33 Gaming board with counters and dice.
34 Clay oil lamp.
35 Bronze drinking vessel.
36 Two-handled two-litre jar.
37 Cooking pot.
38 Samian ware bowl from Gaul.

▽ **Reconstruction of the workshop at Vindolanda.** It was used for leather and woodworking and some of the tools found by the archaeologists are shown on the work-benches. The two men are renewing the bracken with which the hard beaten earth floor was covered. From the evidence of excavations, archaeologists believe that harvesting bracken for floor matting was one of the main activities at Vindolanda, although it was probably only the civilians who did this.

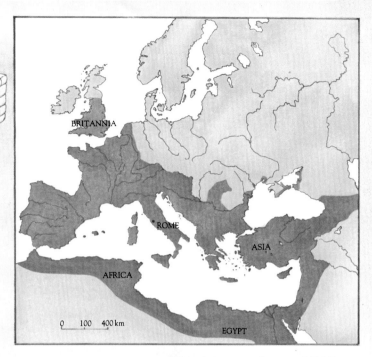

Map showing the extent of the Roman empire at the time of the Emperor Hadrian. Vindolanda, its northernmost outpost, had two periods of particular importance: between AD 163 and 245, and then again from AD 270 to 350. The site was finally abandoned sometime between AD 400 and 500.

The importance of livestock

Animals provided most things necessary for everyday life. As well as transport, food, farming and sport, virtually all clothing came from animal products. Animals also provided the fat for candles, and bone for the handles of knives, and for combs, hair pins, needles, picks, pegs, dice and gaming pieces. Leather was used for buckles, bags, hats, harnesses and tents, as well as for armour and most military and civilian footwear.

Meat was plentiful locally, but cereals were probably brought from the southern regions of Britain; the Wall region was not, and still is not, a good cereal growing area.

Archaeologists have found that hazelnuts collected from the surrounding woods were common in the diet of the fort's inhabitants, and cabbage stalks have been found in the well of the fort.

Local crafts and industry

Although the best pottery was imported, ordinary vessels for everyday use were made locally, some of them at Vindolanda.

Iron was mined and smelted nearby, since the ore was only some 250 metres north of the fort. Coal was also mined and used to heat some civilian homes, although local timber remained the main fuel.

Other industries included bronze-working, weaving and spinning, lime-burning for the making of mortar, leather-tanning and milling.

Within the fort's perimeter there were also repair shops for the implements and tools used in farming, as well as for military equipment.

The Anglo-Saxon invaders

The Anglo-Saxons were people of Germanic stock who lived in northern Germany and Denmark. When the Ostrogoths captured Rome in AD 410 and the Roman empire finally broke up, they started to migrate to Britain. In 450 they arrived in force, driving out the Britons to Cornwall, Wales and Brittany, and establishing seven states: Kent, settled by Jutes; Northumbria, Mercia and East Anglia, settled by Angles; Essex, Sussex and Wessex settled by Saxons.

Anglo-Saxon kings
Each state was ruled by a king. He was the absolute ruler of his own kingdom, although he could at the same time be the subject of a more powerful neighbouring ruler. A king was elected by a council of the greatest lords in the kingdom, but his right to the throne was stronger if he could trace his ancestry back to the founder of the kingdom or even to the gods.

Noblemen
Below the king in the social hierarchy came the nobles. According to Saxon law, a nobleman was a man who had 'land of his own, a church and a kitchen, a bell-house and a castle-gate, a seat and a special office in the king's hall'.

The nobility
1 Nobleman with his falcon. Falconry was a popular sport.
2 Razor.
3 Finely decorated stirrup.
4-5 Two elaborate buckles.
6 Golden brooch.
7 Glass beads were popular.
8 Dress of a well-to-do lady.
9 Toilet scissors.
10 Inscribed gold ring.
11 Silver strainer.
12 Bone comb with its case.
13 Girdle hanger.
14 A simple key.
15-16 Hair pins.
17-18 Two cruciform brooches.

▷During the excavations at Yeavering in Northumberland, an unusual wooden structure was discovered. It was large and shaped rather like a modern grandstand. Its use is uncertain, but may have been used by the king to address his people. The Christian missionary, Paulinus, was at Yeavering in 627 and may also have used it for his preaching.

Christianity
Paulinus, the Christian monk whose work was described by the Venerable Bede in his book *History of the Church and People of England*, was in Northumbria early in the 7th century.
19 Metal clasp from a purse found in the Sutton Hoo ship burial. The figures show the very strong Norse influence which existed in pre-Christian England, particularly in matters of religion.
20 The cross of St Cuthbert, the Northumbrian saint who died in 687 and was buried in Durham.

Yeavering

21 The timber fort at Yeavering, used as a refuge whenever the settlement was attacked.

22 The Great Hall, the most important building at Yeavering, was excavated in 1953-7. First built in 600, it was rebuilt three times that century. Constructed of timber with a thatched roof, the interior was divided by the aisle-posts which also supported the roof. At one end of the hall a partition formed a smaller room separate from the main hall.

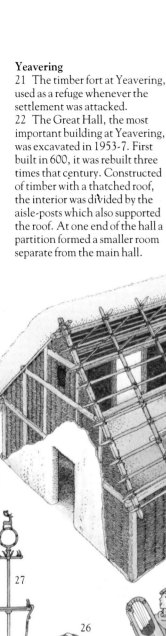

23 A smaller hall which stood near the Great Hall probably housed the king's retinue.

▷ Plan of Yeavering showing the position of the main buildings.

0   50   100 m.

The Sutton Hoo burial

24 Design from a purse found in the tomb of the king buried at Sutton Hoo.

25 Woman playing a lyre of the kind found at Sutton Hoo.

26 Reconstruction of the warrior-king buried at Sutton Hoo in the 7th century. Recent archaeological interpretations suggest a Roman-style outfit with ornaments and weapons of Scandinavian character. Only the most important of kings would have been given such a lavish burial. The quality of the items found in the grave confirm this. They also show that some sectors of society at least were wealthy, since they could afford to bury such expensive items with their dead leader.

27 The iron standard found at Sutton Hoo. It may have been carried at the head of the army in battle.

28 The king's sceptre, a large and decorated whetstone.

29 A Saxon sword.

Royal residences

The finest building in any settlement belonged to the king. The King's Hall, excavated at Yeavering in Northumberland, was the country residence of the kings of Northumbria in early Anglo-Saxon times.

At Yeavering there were several fine timber buildings. The most important was the Great Hall, first built in AD 600, but later rebuilt several times. In King Edwin's reign (616-32) it measured 27 metres long.

Nearby was a larger timber fort in which everyone could take refuge if the settlement was attacked.

Anglo-Saxon settlements

Most Anglo-Saxons lived in villages. The huts of the peasants were grouped around the halls of the king or principal nobleman. On the outskirts of the village, just inside the boundary ditch, were the animal pens.

Most villages were near navigable rivers: the Anglo-Saxons preferred to use waterways rather than the Roman roads. Some well-sited villages grew into market towns, but these were very small by modern standards. Even by AD 1000, York, for example, had no more than 8,000 inhabitants, Lincoln and Norwich 5,000, Thetford 4,000 and Oxford 3,500, and these were the most important towns in the country outside London. The population of the whole of England is estimated to have been only one and a half million.

Christianity

In 597 a mission from Rome, led by Augustine, arrived in Kent to convert the country to Christianity. Within a year the local king, Aethelbert, was converted. Soon the upper classes of the country became Christian, although the peasants took much longer to accept the new religion.

Anglo-Saxon peasants

In the social hierarchy of Anglo-Saxon times, the free peasant came next in rank after the nobleman. He, too, inherited and owned land, had freedom of movement and status in law, but he paid taxes to the king and the church, and had to serve in the army. He co-operated with his neighbours, sharing his ox-team and helping in the fields. But life was tough and a bad harvest often meant hunger and debts.

The unfree man, the slave, was on the lowest social level. He was usually assessed as the equivalent of eight oxen. He could be bought, borrowed, sold or bartered, and had no say in the matter. A man could be born a slave, or could become one through bad luck or debt.

Agriculture

Most of our knowledge of Saxon farming comes from written accounts such as the 11th-century work called *The Wise Reeve*. The land the peasants cultivated was not in a compact holding, but scattered in different fields around the village. Each field was divided into long strips of approximately one acre in area and one 'furlong' in length. 'Furlong' simply means 'one furrow long'. Each villager had to work a number of strips according to how many oxen he contributed to the plough team.

The fields were sown in a three-year cycle of crop rotation. The first field was sown in autumn with corn, perhaps wheat or rye, which grew during the winter. The second field was sown early in the year with barley, beans or oats. The third field was left fallow for a year, and during this time was used as pasture for the livestock who also manured the field. An area was kept as a meadow for hay. This system of cultivation was common in central and northern Europe throughout the Middle Ages.

As well as planting and harvesting the crops, the peasant had to build barns, mend fences, make sheep-pens and fish traps and anything else that needed doing around the village, as instructed by the lord of the manor's bailiff. Refusal could mean a fine, either in money or goods.

Agricultural implements

The tools used by the Saxon peasant were to become the typical tools of the English farmer many years later. The pictures show just how familiar many of them still are to us today. In fact, most tools found in archaeological excavations are identical to modern tools used on modern farms. *The Wise Reeve* lists many tools, including axe, billhook, tughook, mattock, crowbar, ploughshare, coulter, harrow, goad, scythe, sickle, hoe, spade, shovel and rake.

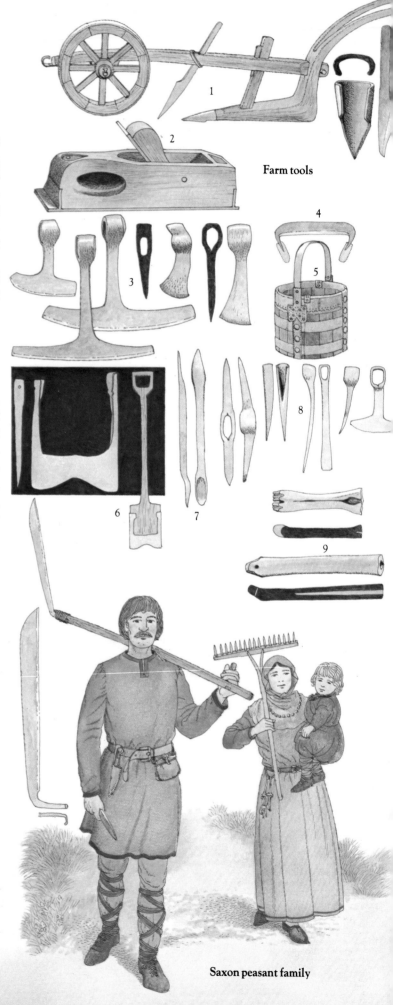

Farm tools

Saxon peasant family

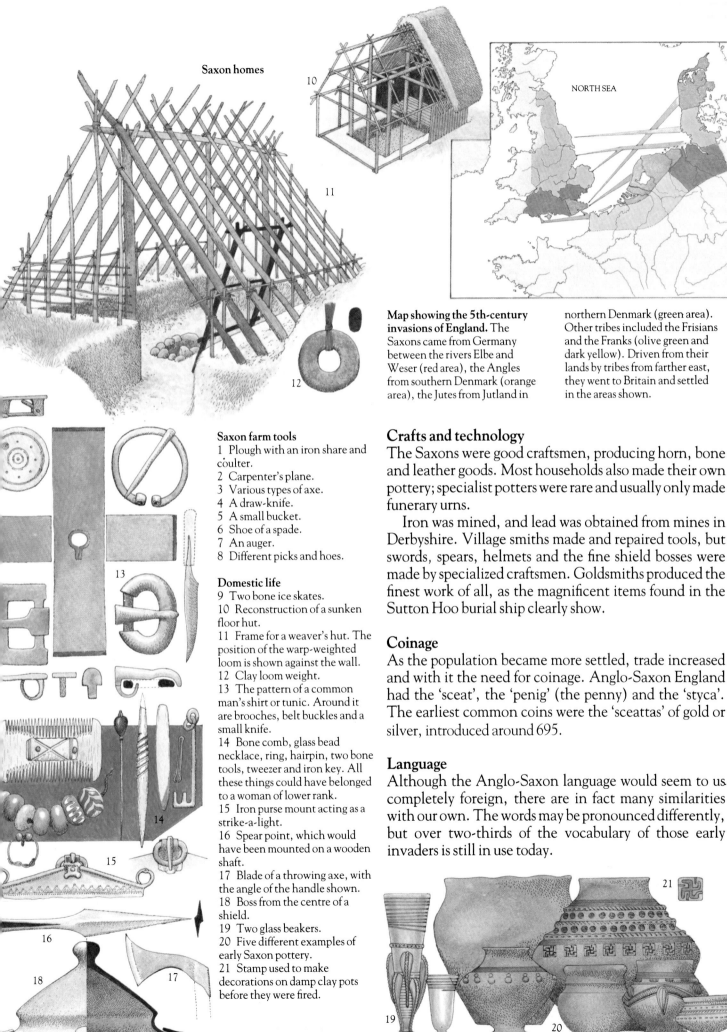

Saxon homes

NORTH SEA

Map showing the 5th-century invasions of England. The Saxons came from Germany between the rivers Elbe and Weser (red area), the Angles from southern Denmark (orange area), the Jutes from Jutland in northern Denmark (green area). Other tribes included the Frisians and the Franks (olive green and dark yellow). Driven from their lands by tribes from farther east, they went to Britain and settled in the areas shown.

Saxon farm tools
1 Plough with an iron share and coulter.
2 Carpenter's plane.
3 Various types of axe.
4 A draw-knife.
5 A small bucket.
6 Shoe of a spade.
7 An auger.
8 Different picks and hoes.

Domestic life
9 Two bone ice skates.
10 Reconstruction of a sunken floor hut.
11 Frame for a weaver's hut. The position of the warp-weighted loom is shown against the wall.
12 Clay loom weight.
13 The pattern of a common man's shirt or tunic. Around it are brooches, belt buckles and a small knife.
14 Bone comb, glass bead necklace, ring, hairpin, two bone tools, tweezer and iron key. All these things could have belonged to a woman of lower rank.
15 Iron purse mount acting as a strike-a-light.
16 Spear point, which would have been mounted on a wooden shaft.
17 Blade of a throwing axe, with the angle of the handle shown.
18 Boss from the centre of a shield.
19 Two glass beakers.
20 Five different examples of early Saxon pottery.
21 Stamp used to make decorations on damp clay pots before they were fired.

Crafts and technology

The Saxons were good craftsmen, producing horn, bone and leather goods. Most households also made their own pottery; specialist potters were rare and usually only made funerary urns.

Iron was mined, and lead was obtained from mines in Derbyshire. Village smiths made and repaired tools, but swords, spears, helmets and the fine shield bosses were made by specialized craftsmen. Goldsmiths produced the finest work of all, as the magnificent items found in the Sutton Hoo burial ship clearly show.

Coinage

As the population became more settled, trade increased and with it the need for coinage. Anglo-Saxon England had the 'sceat', the 'penig' (the penny) and the 'styca'. The earliest common coins were the 'sceattas' of gold or silver, introduced around 695.

Language

Although the Anglo-Saxon language would seem to us completely foreign, there are in fact many similarities with our own. The words may be pronounced differently, but over two-thirds of the vocabulary of those early invaders is still in use today.

Byzantium: the new Rome

Justinian

In AD 311 the Roman empire was in a state of confusion, with four rulers all claiming the title of emperor. By 323 Constantine had emerged as victor. But, after the years of unrest in Rome, he decided to move the capital of the empire to a safer place. In 330 he chose Byzantium, an ancient and relatively unimportant Greek city, but with a good trading position in the eastern Mediterranean. He intended to call his new capital 'Second Rome', but the name 'Constantinople' (City of Constantine) was more popular. Today the city is called Istanbul.

The Byzantine empire, with its capital at Constantinople, was the Roman empire of the East. It kept alive Roman culture and traditions long after Rome had fallen into the hands of barbarian invaders and its empire destroyed. The new eastern empire lasted over a thousand years. It became the main Mediterranean power and was the most brilliant culture in the so-called 'Dark Ages', until the city's final capture by the Turks in 1453.

Christianity

Constantine, who was a convert to Christianity, legalized the religion throughout the empire. He started a great building programme in Constantinople, and over the years many fine churches were built.

One of the finest was Hagia Sophia, started by the Emperor Justinian in 537. The church, with its great domes symbolizing heaven, towered over all other buildings in the city. The vaulted interior, over 30 metres across and 60 metres high, was the largest of any church in Europe.

Civil laws

One of the most important contributions made by the Byzantine empire to our own civilization was the transmission of Roman law. In 528 Justinian, the greatest Byzantine emperor, appointed a commission of ten men to clarify and edit the laws of the various Roman emperors. As a result, the civil laws of Byzantium were properly codified, and Roman law was preserved.

Scenes of Byzantine life
1 The Emperor Justinian on his carved ivory throne with the Empress Theodora. A royal guard stands behind them.
2 Young lady's headdress.
3 A lady courtier.
4 Young man of the court. His toga was much simpler than that worn by the Romans.

5 Archbishop Maximianus of the court of Justinian.
6 Cavalryman's uniform, with spear and round shield.
7 The emperor as a cavalryman.
8 An infantryman in uniform, with spear, bow, scaled armour and oval shield.
The costumes are shown on mosaics in Ravenna.

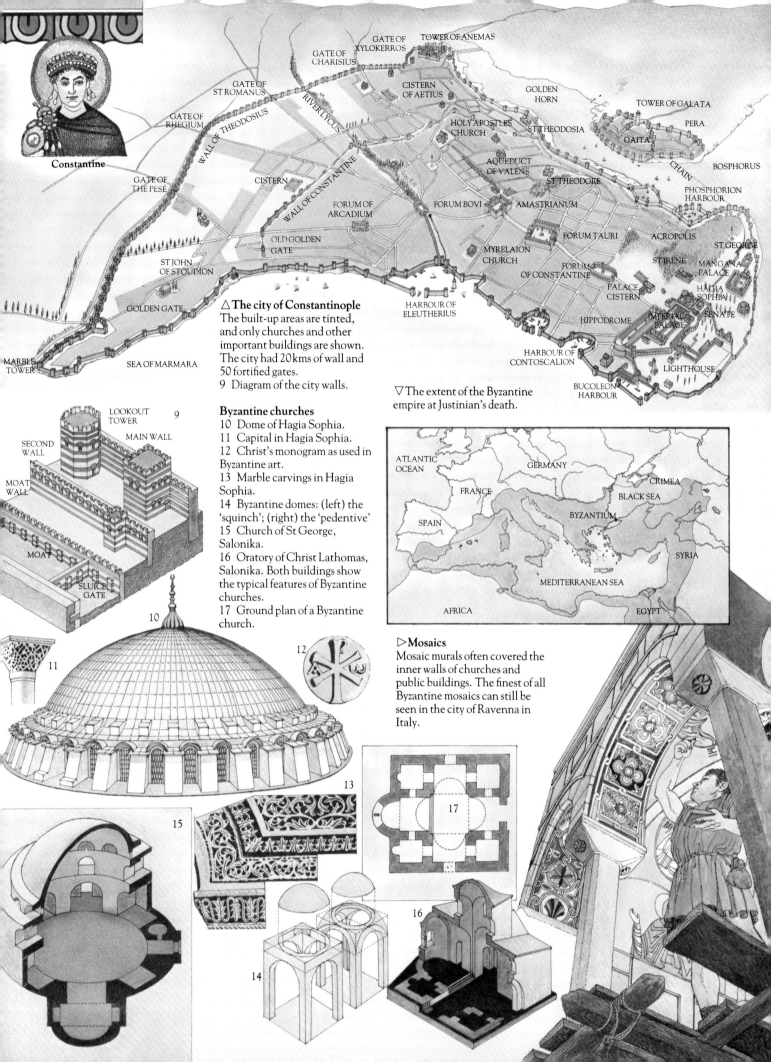

Constantine

GATE OF XYLOKERROS
TOWER OF ANEMAS
GATE OF CHARISIUS
GATE OF ST ROMANUS
GATE OF RHEGIUM
WALL OF THEODOSIUS
RIVER LYCUS
CISTERN OF AETIUS
GOLDEN HORN
TOWER OF GALATA
PERA
GAITA
CHAIN
BOSPHORUS
HOLY APOSTLES CHURCH
ST THEODOSIA
AQUEDUCT OF VALENS
ST THEODORE
PHOSPHORION HARBOUR
GATE OF THE PESÉ
CISTERN
WALL OF CONSTANTINE
FORUM OF ARCADIUM
FORUM BOVI
AMASTRIANUM
FORUM TAURI
ACROPOLIS
ST GEORGE
OLD GOLDEN GATE
MYRELAION CHURCH
FORUM OF CONSTANTINE
ST IRENE
MANGANA PALACE
ST JOHN OF STOUDION
PALACE CISTERN
HAGIA SOPHIA
SENATE
GOLDEN GATE
HARBOUR OF ELEUTHERIUS
HIPPODROME
IMPERIAL PALACE
MARBLE TOWER
SEA OF MARMARA
HARBOUR OF CONTOSCALION
LIGHTHOUSE
BUCOLEON HARBOUR

△ **The city of Constantinople**
The built-up areas are tinted, and only churches and other important buildings are shown. The city had 20 kms of wall and 50 fortified gates.
9 Diagram of the city walls.

▽ The extent of the Byzantine empire at Justinian's death.

Byzantine churches
10 Dome of Hagia Sophia.
11 Capital in Hagia Sophia.
12 Christ's monogram as used in Byzantine art.
13 Marble carvings in Hagia Sophia.
14 Byzantine domes: (left) the 'squinch'; (right) the 'pedentive'
15 Church of St George, Salonika.
16 Oratory of Christ Lathomas, Salonika. Both buildings show the typical features of Byzantine churches.
17 Ground plan of a Byzantine church.

LOOKOUT TOWER 9
MAIN WALL
SECOND WALL
MOAT WALL
MOAT
SLUICE GATE

ATLANTIC OCEAN
GERMANY
CRIMEA
FRANCE
BLACK SEA
SPAIN
BYZANTIUM
SYRIA
MEDITERRANEAN SEA
AFRICA
EGYPT

▷ **Mosaics**
Mosaic murals often covered the inner walls of churches and public buildings. The finest of all Byzantine mosaics can still be seen in the city of Ravenna in Italy.

Byzantine art and architecture

The Byzantine empire is probably best-known today for its marvellous artistic tradition. This showed the influence of Greek and Roman styles, but also developed a distinct character of its own, particularly in religious art and architecture which, in turn, influenced every nation that came into contact with it.

The Bucoleon palace

One of the outstanding palaces built by Constantine was the Bucoleon, which overlooked the imperial harbour. This palace was one of seven royal residences and consisted of a series of buildings and gardens. Brightly coloured mosaics and marble ornamented the pavilions, fountains and pools. Around 20,000 civil servants were employed at the palace, together with guards, entertainers, courtiers and clergy. In the palace workshops scores of craftsmen made weapons, dyes and precious silks. These were state monopolies, and the profits from them supported the state bureaucracy.

Crafts

The palace was not the only place which had craft workshops. In towns and cities throughout the empire there were thousands of craftsmen.

Craft activities were strictly controlled by law. Workshops could only be set up in streets and arcades chosen by the city prefect. Specialized skills were encouraged. Guilds set standards, specified materials and punished bad workmanship. As a result, traders from the rest of the world flocked to Byzantine cities to buy the fine quality goods.

Trade

The merchants who came to the cities to buy also brought with them goods to sell, and Constantinople in particular became an important trading centre.

Gold, silver, precious stones and silks arrived in the city from India, Persia and China. Ivory from elephant tusks also came from India and, after the 9th century, walrus ivory from the Arctic was brought by the Vikings.

Shipping

As trade developed, so did shipping. The Byzantine cargo ship shown opposite was built in the 7th century. It was 55 metres long at the waterline; and when it sank off the Turkish coast it was carrying a cargo of over 900 amphorae.

Constantinople's geographical position (see page 25) made it a good trading port, with many sheltered harbours along the Golden Horn and Sea of Marmara.

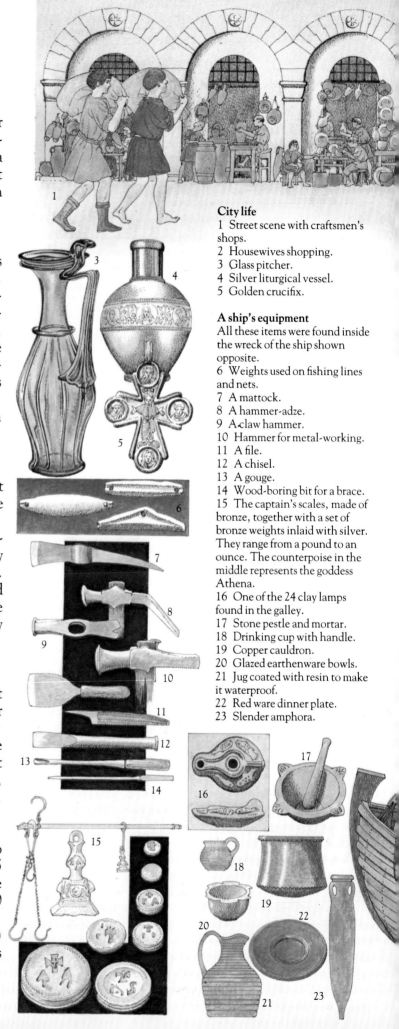

City life
1 Street scene with craftsmen's shops.
2 Housewives shopping.
3 Glass pitcher.
4 Silver liturgical vessel.
5 Golden crucifix.

A ship's equipment
All these items were found inside the wreck of the ship shown opposite.
6 Weights used on fishing lines and nets.
7 A mattock.
8 A hammer-adze.
9 A claw hammer.
10 Hammer for metal-working.
11 A file.
12 A chisel.
13 A gouge.
14 Wood-boring bit for a brace.
15 The captain's scales, made of bronze, together with a set of bronze weights inlaid with silver. They range from a pound to an ounce. The counterpoise in the middle represents the goddess Athena.
16 One of the 24 clay lamps found in the galley.
17 Stone pestle and mortar.
18 Drinking cup with handle.
19 Copper cauldron.
20 Glazed earthenware bowls.
21 Jug coated with resin to make it waterproof.
22 Red ware dinner plate.
23 Slender amphora.

2

24

25

A mixed population
The merchants who thronged
the streets of Byzantine cities
included Jews, Italians, Russians,
Greeks, Bulgars, Armenians and
Kazars. Even the Vikings reached
Constantinople in the 9th
century.

A merchant ship
24 Pictures of Byzantine cargo
ships from the mosaics at
Ravenna.
25 Archaeologist's
reconstruction of one of these
cargo ships.
26 Sections through the ship.

26

BOW

Plans of a Byzantine cargo ship

STERN

STEERING-OAR

SMOKE HOLE

STERN

HATCHES

GALLEY ROOF
COVERED WITH
ROOFING TILES

HEARTH MADE
OF CERAMIC TILES

GALLEY FLOOR

STORAGE SPACE

HOLD

The Arabs in Europe

Islam is the religion based on the teachings of the prophet Mohammed (570-632). A Muslim (follower of Mohammed) is under five obligations: 1 The confession of faith ('There is no God but Allah and Mohammed is his Prophet'); 2 Prayers five times a day; 3 Charitable gifts (usually taxes to the state); 4 The fast in the month of Ramadhan; 5 The pilgrimage to Mecca at least once in a lifetime.

A growing faith

While the Saxons were establishing themselves in England and the Byzantine empire was thriving, in the arid peninsula of Arabia the teachings of Mohammed and the Islamic faith were spreading. After his death his followers continued to preach and conquer in the name of Islam. By 715 the Muslim empire stretched from the Indus region of modern Pakistan in the east to Spain in the west.

This remarkably swift conquest of most of the Near East and Mediterranean region was partly because many peoples in these regions were oppressed by their rulers and accepted the Arab armies as liberators.

Having conquered most of Spain by 714, the Arabs looked north to France and the rest of Europe. They carried out many attacks across the Pyrenees, but in 732 were defeated in a battle with the Frankish army at a place between Tours and Poitiers. Europe's history would have been very different if they had won that battle!

Arab writing
1 'Mashq', an early Arabic script (700-50).
2 Writing implements. The scissors were used to cut scrolls.
3 An Arab bookcase.
4 The 'Kufic' script.
5 The 'Naskhi' script which replaced Kufic in the 10th century.
6 A scribe writes on a scroll as a scholar dictates to him.

Arab seafaring
7 Vessel used by Arab traders in the Mediterranean. The triangular sail was called a 'lateen'.

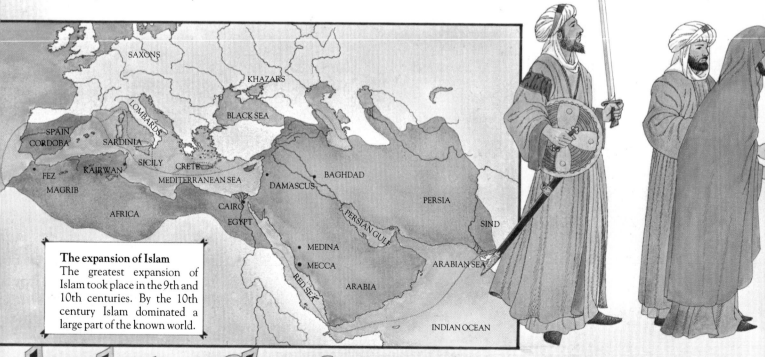

The expansion of Islam
The greatest expansion of Islam took place in the 9th and 10th centuries. By the 10th century Islam dominated a large part of the known world.

Arab science

8 A chemist in his shop. Arab science incorporated the experience of the Greeks, and also that of Persia and India. This knowledge was transmitted to Europe through Spain and Sicily.

9 A 13th-century astrolabe from Cordoba. Travellers used them to find their direction from the position of the stars.

8

9

▽ **A nomad's tent.** The population of Arabia consisted of tribes of Bedouin whose nomadic way of life was suited to the desert climate.

(bottom) **A caliph** with his army and standard bearers consulting a local vizir. There are few pictures of Arab costume of this period, and the drawing is reconstructed from the few available sources.

▷ **Arab mosques**

10 Minaret of the Great Mosque at Kairwan, Tunisia. The lower part of the minaret is part of an older mosque which dated to 724. The upper portions date from 836, as does the rest of the mosque.

11 The spiralled, or staged, minaret of the Great Mosque at Samarra in Iraq, built in 848. The mosque is the largest in the Islamic world. Although now in ruins, it was once a splendid example of Islamic architecture and art.

New rulers, new influences

After conquest came consolidation. The Arabs had a much higher standard of living than most European peoples at this time, as so many of their artefacts clearly show. Their ceramics were particularly fine, using techniques unknown in the west, such as underglaze painting and slip-painting.

The designs and patterns the Muslim craftsmen introduced were very beautiful and enormously influenced later European arts. The 'arabesque', for example, is a stylized plant scroll pattern developed from the classical vine. It was used in various forms to adorn buildings, pottery, carpets, manuscripts and many other objects.

Arab scholars at this time also laid the foundations of the modern sciences of mathematics, medicine and astronomy, knowledge which was to be of great benefit to Europe and European scholars.

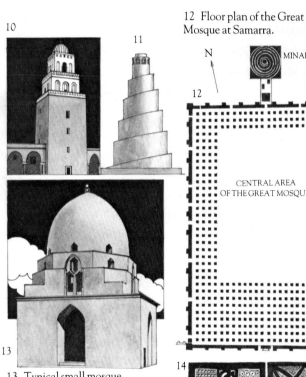

10

11

12 Floor plan of the Great Mosque at Samarra.

N

MINARET

12

CENTRAL AREA OF THE GREAT MOSQUE

13

13 Typical small mosque.

14

Decorative styles

14 Different patterns on lustre tiles from the mosque at Kairwan.
15 Ceiling panel from the mosque, showing a typical pattern and display of colours.
16 Stucco wall panel from the mosque at Samarra.
17 Gold and brown lustre bowl from Samarra dating from the 9th century. It was through the Arabs that glazed pottery came to be widely used in Europe. Craftsmen passed on the techniques and merchants brought them to northern markets.

16

15

17

Cordoba – Arabia in Spain

Cordoba, the most important centre of Muslim influence in Spain, was already large before the Arabs conquered it, but under them it developed rapidly. In the 10th century, at the height of Arab rule, it had a population of 500,000. It had 113,000 houses, 700 mosques and 300 public baths. These, together with its 70 libraries, bookshops and university, made it the most civilized place in the western world, and probably the largest city. No town in Europe at this time had more than 10,000 inhabitants and most were much smaller (see page 21 for population figures in England in early medieval times).

The Great Mosque

Mosques were the Muslim churches. The Great Mosque at Cordoba still stands just as it did in the network of streets within the city's wall. Although mosques were first and foremost centres of worship, they were also meeting places for travellers and even for local people who wished to escape the heat of the streets in the summer.

Houses and homes

The houses of Cordoba were similar to Arab houses in North Africa and the Middle East. Poorer houses had walls of unfired bricks dried in the sun, but there were also many larger houses belonging to wealthy merchants and officials. These often had two storeys, gardens and their own water supply contained within their high walls. Outside, the walls of the houses looked plain and dull, with few windows and balconies covered with lattice-work screens. Inside, however, cool comfortable rooms surrounded a central courtyard. Often a fountain and flowers added to the general feeling of peacefulness.

Furniture was sparse. People sat on carpets and cushions or outside in the garden. At mealtimes all the courses were served at once and everyone helped themselves as they pleased. Although drinking wine is forbidden in the Koran, this rule was largely ignored in Spain.

The end of Arab domination

From around 1014 rebellions and civil war spread across Muslim-dominated Spain. In 1031 the Caliphate of Cordoba came to an end, but out of its ruins many small kingdoms arose. There was much fighting between these kingdoms, to the advantage of the Christians who set up states in the north of Spain and, gradually pushing southward, overthrew the last stronghold of the Muslims in Europe in 1492 – the year in which Columbus discovered America and claimed it for his patrons: the king and queen of Spain.

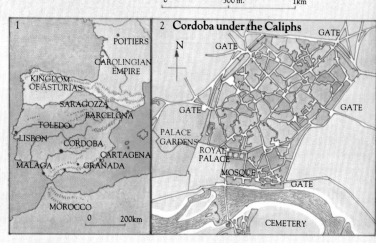

Arab coin

The Arab influence

1 The Muslim empire in Spain around 714 when at its greatest extent.

2 Plan of Cordoba under the Muslims. Many of the streets were paved and lit, something quite unknown in the rest of Europe.

3 Surgical instruments which illustrated an Arab manuscript. The Muslims' medical knowledge was far in advance of that of the Europeans of the time. Abulcasis was outstanding among many learned Arab doctors, and became famous in medieval Europe.

4 The Arabs introduced new numbers to replace the old Roman ones. Shown here are

A Arabic
B Spanish
C Italian.

Decorative styles

5 Wall painting from Cairo showing the costume and style of painting which was introduced into Italy by the Arab conquerors.

The Arabs liked luxury goods and were extremely fine craftsmen. They brought many new techniques with them to the lands they conquered.

6 An ivory 'oliphant' or drinking horn made in southern Italy.

7 Decorative earthenware jar made in Egypt.

8 Sicilian-Muslim ivory box.

◁ **The Great Mosque at Cordoba**, a fine example of Muslim architecture.

9 The mosque's central dome, with its series of inter-crossing arches, seen from below.

10 Detail of the façade of the mosque from above the main entrance.

11 Kufic script from a wall inside the mosque.

12 Plan of the mosque's main entrance.

13 Marble screen from a window in the mosque.

An Arab house

14 Reconstruction of a house in Cordoba which probably belonged to a merchant in the 10th century. Rooms open off the paved central courtyard in which is a fountain and well. Above is a covered gallery.

15 11th-century marble well from Toledo.

16 Door lock still common in the Muslim world.

17 Three types of oil lamp from Muslim Palermo, Sicily.

Home life

18 Lute, an instrument popular with the Arabs which they introduced into the lands they conquered.

19 Tambourine, another musical instrument introduced into Europe by the Arabs.

20 Reconstruction of a scene from a wealthy Arab home (based on a 10th-century carved ivory casket). Musicians entertain members of the family and their friends and a servant brings refreshments. Falconry was a very popular sport among men from rich families. Well-trained birds fetched high prices.

21 Ivory casket of Hispano-Arabic style from Cordoba (960-70) showing a hunting scene.

22 Ovens for baking the unleavened Muslim bread.

The Vikings

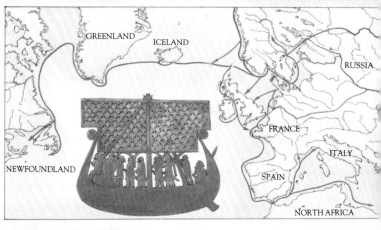

In the ancient Norse language of Scandinavia a 'vik' was a creek, an inlet or a bay. The Vikings may have got their name because they were pirates who lay hidden in a vik waiting for a merchant vessel to pass by. This particular theory on the origin of their name well fits the character of these ancient Scandinavians as reported by contemporary historians and chroniclers.

The peoples of Scandinavia were of Germanic stock, related to the Anglo-Saxons and to the other peoples settled around the North Sea and Baltic, and in Germany.

Seafarers and travellers

According to historians, it was overpopulation of their lands in about AD 800 that made the Scandinavian peoples turn to the sea to seek out new territories. Whatever the cause, they were certainly successful; they travelled far and reached countries that no European had reached before. Indeed, it would be many centuries before their exploits were matched again.

Ships for the seafarers

The Vikings' travels were made possible by the keeled long ship. This had a reinforced bottom for the keel and mast, and was much more efficient than the old oared boat. The most common of the Viking ships, especially along the Atlantic coasts, were the merchant ships. Built for cargo capacity and seaworthiness, they may not have had the speed and manoeuvrability of the long ships used by the Vikings in war, but they were excellent for transport over long distances. It was in ships such as these that the Vikings reached and colonized new lands, including America almost five centuries before Columbus.

Plunderers and colonizers

Although they were all of Germanic origin, the peoples from different parts of Scandinavia formed distinct groups and this is reflected in the different directions they went in their voyages of plunder and colonization.

The Danish Vikings attacked the coasts of France, Spain and Portugal and even reached Italy. In Britain, they overran Northumbria and East Anglia.

The Norwegian Vikings occupied the Orkneys, the Shetlands, the Hebrides and Ireland. They settled in Iceland and Greenland, and founded a colony in Newfoundland in 1000.

The Swedish Vikings went eastwards. They followed the great rivers of Russia through eastern Europe, and reached the eastern Mediterranean and Constantinople, which they attacked unsuccessfully in 860.

△ **Map** showing the main land and sea routes taken by the Vikings, c. AD 1000. Inset is a representation of a Viking ship under sail, taken from a carving on a tombstone.

▽ **Viking shipbuilder** at work. Around him are shown some of the many tools used by the Vikings in the construction and decoration of their ships.

The Oseberg ship (bottom) was used as a tomb for a Viking queen in the 9th century. It was excavated in Norway in 1904, and remains one of the outstanding examples of Viking craftsmanship.
(below) Detail of part of the carving on the Oseberg ship.

The Oseberg ship

The Gokstad ship

The Gokstad ship was excavated in southern Norway in 1880. Although smaller than the ships used by the Vikings to raid western Europe, it was much larger and sturdier than the Oseberg ship shown opposite. The keel was cut from one piece of oak for almost its whole length of 23 m. The sides were also of oak, 16 planks on each side. The keel was joined to the prow and stern posts, which were made out of curved oak.

1-4 Four different views of the ship.

5 The anchor.

6 Type of rigging block found with the ship.

7 One of the wooden flaps which covered the ship's oar-holes to prevent water entering when the oars were withdrawn.

8 Another type of rigging block used on the ship. As no rigging remains, it is hard to know how the block was used.

9 The ship was rowed with 16 pairs of oars; each oar was 5.55 m. long. When the ship was found there was nothing for the oarsmen to have sat on. They either rowed standing up, or sat on stools which were removed before the ship was buried.

10 The ship's rudder. It was large, 3.27 m. long and 56 cm wide, and was attached to the last rib of the rear section of the ship (A).

11 One of the round-headed nails with an inner riveted tip used to join the planks of the keel together.

12 Ship's weather vane which was placed on top of the mast. No sails survive from Viking times, although there are plenty of carvings showing ships with one square sail.

13 Ship's bearing dial, reconstructed from a fragment found in Greenland.

The Gokstad ship

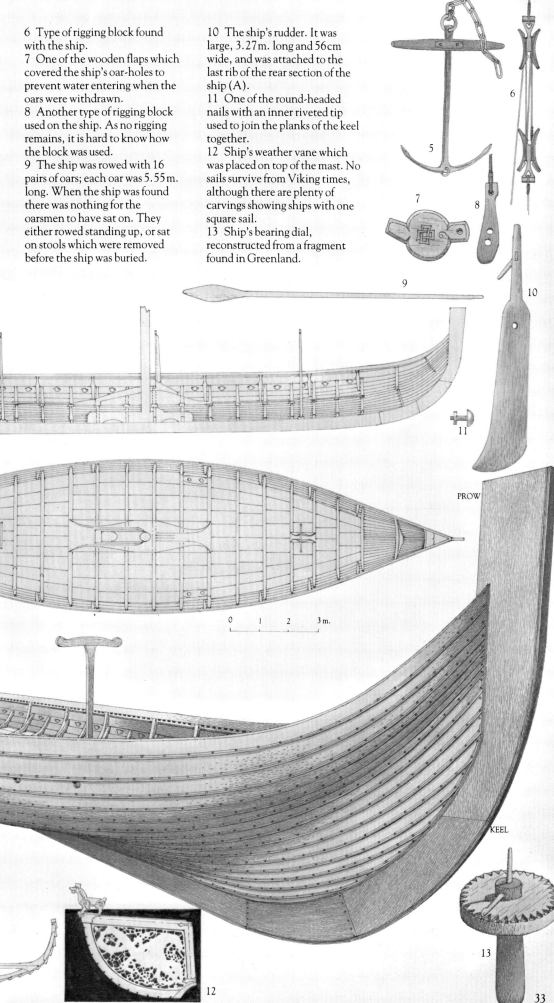

33

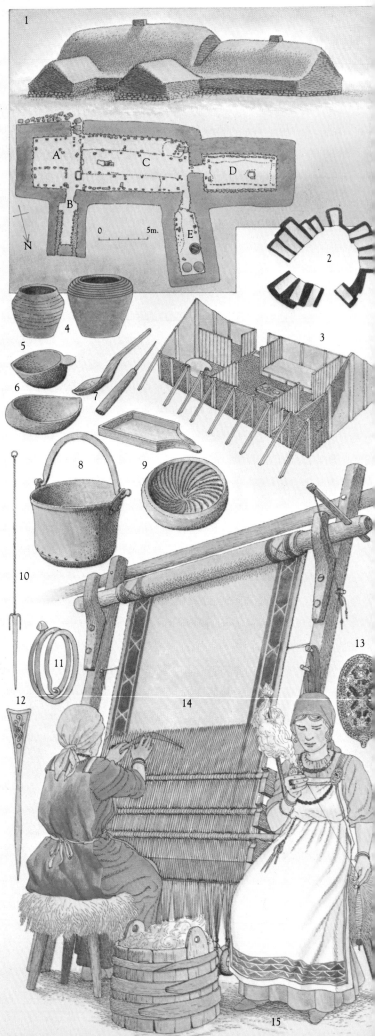

Viking culture

Although the Vikings are mostly remembered today for their plundering of defenceless towns and monasteries, they were also fine craftsmen. If their boats had not been well-made, for example, they would never have survived the long sea journeys.

In Roman times the peoples of Scandinavia had had contact with the more sophisticated way of life in southern Europe, and knew, through trade, of Roman products and crafts. By AD 1000 they had evolved their own style of workmanship and decoration.

Like most European peoples of the time, the majority of the Vikings could not read or write, but they were certainly not an illiterate people. As well as their great sagas, which were part of an ancient oral tradition, they had their own alphabet, the runic alphabet, which was in use in AD 200. Runic letters were rather angular, more suited to carving with a knife on wood or stone than writing on a parchment scroll with pen and ink. The alphabet had similarities with that of the Etruscans and early Greeks.

The structure of Viking society

Viking society was at first rather fluid and fragmented. Later, however, it developed into the feudal structure that was common throughout Europe at the time. At the top was the king or most powerful of the noblemen. Next came the aristocrats, the chieftains. They were warriors and often held their lands by force. Later, when their society became more settled, these men held land from the king. Then came the free peasants – though if they had once been slaves or belonged to a slave family, they were never entirely free. At the very bottom of the scale were the slaves. They could be bought and sold by their masters just like any other sort of merchandise.

Viking homes
1 Reconstruction of a 10th-century farmhouse at Stöng, Iceland: A entrance hall; B pantry; C main hall; D smaller hall; E dairy. The turf walls were on stone footings.
2 Complex of houses around a central courtyard, Norway.
3 Reconstruction of a Viking house in southern Denmark.
4 Kitchen pots from Sweden.
5-7 Wooden utensils.
8 Iron cauldron.
9 Soapstone bowl.
10 Iron spit for cooking meat.
11 Silver bracelet.
12 Decorated bone hairpin.
13 Decorated bronze brooch.

Weaving
14 A Viking loom can be reconstructed because similar ones were used in Iceland until the 19th century. Like the looms of the Celts and Saxons it was warp weighted. Working from the top downwards, the weaver passed the weft (horizontal) threads through those of the vertical warp.
15 Spinning wool into thread so that it can be woven into cloth. The spinner wears a brooch similar to 13.
Both these women would have belonged to fairly wealthy families. Poorer women would have worn plainer clothes.

Household goods

16 Early 9th-century silver coin made in Denmark.
17 Balance scales and decorated weights.
18 Runic stone from Sweden.
19 Woollen stocking-breeches with belt loops at the waist.
20 Woollen hood from Greenland.
21 Fisherman's line winder.
22 Decorated leather belt end.
23 Leather ankle boot.
24 Brooch used to fasten a man's cloak.

25 Early Viking helmet from a grave in Sweden.
26 Viking warrior.
27 Agricultural implements: A scythe and sickle blades; B ploughshare; C spike used for horses' feet when crossing ice.
28 Silver pendant in the form of Thor's hammer. It was also the symbol of a Viking smith or swordmaker.

The Viking smith
29 Heads of battle axes.
30 Decorative sword hilts.
31 Spear heads from Sweden.
32 A Viking sword.
33 Viking smith at work.

34 The runic alphabet.
35 Stone with an inscription in runic lettering recording the landing of the Vikings on an island off Greenland, 1330.

△ **The Viking age in Scandinavia.** Red: Viking Norway; green: Viking Sweden; yellow: Viking Denmark. The boundaries between the Viking nations were not strictly defined, and settlements were mostly limited to the more accessible and fertile regions. The dotted lines indicate the frontiers of the modern states of Norway, Sweden and Denmark.

Agriculture

Contrary to popular belief, most Scandinavian peoples never went to sea. Instead they worked on the land, growing crops and rearing animals. If, as historians believe, it was overpopulation that caused the Vikings to become plunderers, this would suggest that they were also successful farmers.

Most Vikings seem to have lived on isolated farms. This was certainly the case in Iceland and Greenland. On these farms they reared cattle, horses, sheep and goats, which provided meat, milk, transport and clothing. In winter the animals were kept near the farms, but in summer they were driven up to the high mountain pastures.

Fishing was another important source of food. The chief agricultural crops were barley and oats. Hay was grown as fodder for the animals.

Religion

Like the ancient Greeks and Romans, the Vikings worshipped numerous gods. Each god governed one aspect of life. Odin was the chief god; he was all-wise, but was also the god of war. Thor, whose symbol was the hammer, was the protector of the peasants. Vikings who settled in Britain, Ireland and Normandy quickly adopted Christianity.

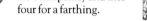

△ Silver penny, cut in two for a halfpenny and into four for a farthing.

Castle and manor house

Castles were unknown in England until introduced by the Normans in the 11th century. A castle was the feudal lord's fortified residence from which he dominated the surrounding countryside. This system was new in England; the earlier British hilltop forts and the fortified towns of the Saxons had been for the defence of the community.

The Normans when they first invaded England hurriedly put up earth and timber forts, mostly of the simple 'motte and bailey' type shown below. Later they used stone and built strong square-towered castles. These were superseded, in turn, by castles with round keeps which, unlike the square ones, had no blind spots of which attackers could take advantage.

A medieval nobleman's household

The household of a medieval nobleman was partly military and partly administrative. Under his command the lord had knights, men at arms, archers and crossbowmen, night watchmen, stable marshals and gatekeepers. Not all lived permanently in the castle. It was cheaper to call them up from their own homes whenever necessary.

The head of the domestic side of the castle was the steward. He was responsible for the running of the castle and its estates.

The castle hall

The great hall was the centre of the castle's life. It served as living and sleeping quarters for everyone except the lord and his family. Now that there was a wooden upper floor, the traditional central hearth of the Saxon hall was no longer safe, so the fire was moved to one side of the hall.

(top left) Seal of Henry II. In days when few were literate, seals were important to show a document was genuine.

The knight on his warhorse
1 Helmet with nose-piece.
2 Lances.
3 Snaffle bit for draught and packhorses.
4 Battle axe.
5 Detail of chain mail.
6 Each link of mail was individually riveted.
7 Arrowheads.
8 A knight's heavy sword.
9 Dagger with leather sheath.
10 Whetstone for sharpening blades.
11 Long shield for a knight.
12 Putting on mail armour.
13 Stirrup.
14 Prick spur worn by knights.
15 Horse-shoe.
16 Crossbow. The bow string was pulled over a nut which released it when the trigger handle was pulled (A).
17 Trebuchet, a weapon used in sieges to hurl stones over walls.
18 'Motte and bailey' type of castle.
19 Orford Castle, Suffolk, with a reconstruction of its bailey.

'Motte and bailey' castle

Orford Castle

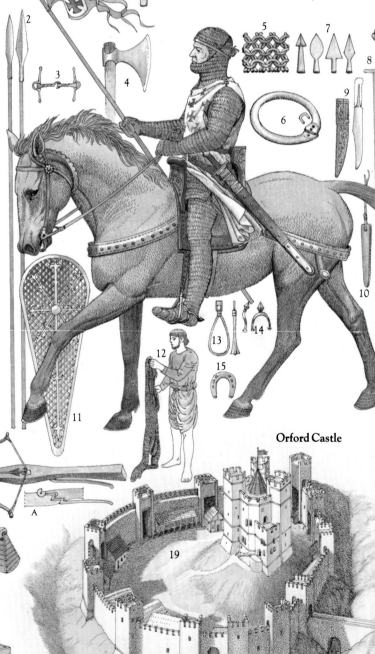

20 NORTH TOWER

OVEN

STAIRCASE TURRET

GUARD ROOM

CISTERN

SECOND FLOOR HALL

KITCHEN

GARDEROBE

CHAPLAIN'S CHAMBER

GARDEROBE

FIRST FLOOR HALL

CHAPEL

KITCHEN

VESTIBULE

ENTRANCE

BASEMENT

GARDEROBES

PRISON

The lord and his lady at home

20 Exploded diagram of the central keep and living quarters of a castle.

21 Baggage waggon.

22 Padded horse collar. These enabled horses to pull much heavier loads.

23 Canopied bed for the lord. Curtains might also be hung around it for warmth and privacy. Retainers slept on benches in the hall.

24 Metal pen and ivory pen case. The lord's clerical work was done by his chaplain.

25 Hanging oil lamp for use in the chapel. Elsewhere simpler oil lamps or candles stuck on iron spikes were used.

26 Wooden aumbrey for storing valuable possessions. Sometimes aumbries were recessed into the masonry of a wall.

27 Silver mounted ivory casket.

28 Spoons of bone and silver. People brought their own knife and spoon to the table. They were kept in a container hanging from the belt or girdle.

29 Metal tap head.

30 Rings set with stones.

31 Musicians, drawn from a manuscript: A playing the harp; B chiming bells; C a rebec.

32 A wealthy noble and his family. The chair he is sitting on could be dismantled for easy transport. Chairs were a status symbol and were reserved for the most important persons present.

33 Earthenware cooking pots.

34 Earthenware dish.

35 Bronze aquamanile used for washing the hands before meals.

37

The manorial estate

The economic basis of the feudal system was the manorial estate. In its very simplest form it consisted of one village with one lord (though the lord might own many manors). Part of the estate was reserved for the lord, and was his 'demesne'. The rest was farmed partly by freemen who paid rents for their land, and partly by 'villeins'. These latter could not leave the manor, and in return for their land they had to work for two or three days each week on the lord's demesne, with extra days at busy times like haymaking and harvest. Villeins also had to give their lords eggs, chickens, pigs, butter and other produce as rent for their land.

These rents were always unpopular, but the restriction most disliked by both freemen and villeins was the enforced use of the lord's mill. There was usually only one mill in a village and it was owned by the lord. The villagers who wanted to have their corn ground into flour were forced to use the lord's mill, and to pay for the privilege. It is hardly surprising, therefore, that in the stories of the time, millers are usually portrayed as dishonest, unpopular figures!

A small country manor

By 1200 many manor houses were built of stone. Some of these have survived, although the surrounding buildings which were not stone-built have long since disappeared and can only be reconstructed.

On the manor's ground floor were the cellars and storerooms, and the main hall was on the first floor. The hall was occupied by the bailiff, the lord's permanent representative on the manor. When the lord or his steward arrived, to hold the manor court or audit the accounts, the bailiff moved into one of the other buildings nearby.

Life for the peasant

The small one-roomed houses of the peasants were strung along the village street, each one in a small plot of land. This was the only land in the village which the villein could cultivate exactly as he liked. He usually grew fruit or vegetables to increase his family's food supply.

The rest of his land was scattered throughout the common fields of the manor. This system had originated in Saxon times and the Normans did little to interfere with it. So, for the peasant, life continued largely unchanged. He continued to farm his strips under the direction of the 'reeve', a peasant overseer who was elected each year by the other peasants.

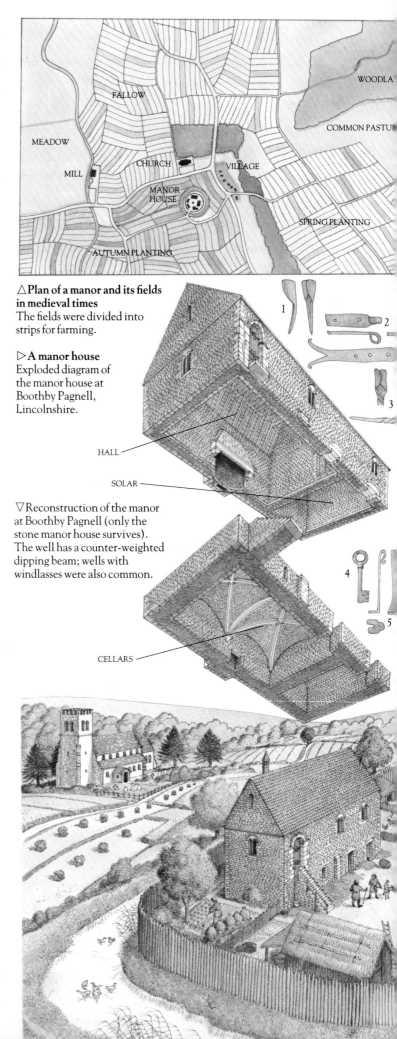

△ **Plan of a manor and its fields in medieval times**
The fields were divided into strips for farming.

▷ **A manor house**
Exploded diagram of the manor house at Boothby Pagnell, Lincolnshire.

HALL

SOLAR

▽ Reconstruction of the manor at Boothby Pagnell (only the stone manor house survives). The well has a counter-weighted dipping beam; wells with windlasses were also common.

CELLARS

Household objects from the manorial estate

1 Socketed iron candleholder.
2 Door hinges.
3 Another type of candleholder.
4 Iron door key.
5 Padlock key, three views.
6 Earthenware pitcher.
7 Earthenware dishes.
8 Tall earthenware pitcher for carrying liquids.
9-11 Three different types of cresset lamp. These were filled with oil and a wick inserted for burning.
12 Money-box with a slit just big enough for a silver penny.
13 Curfew which was put over the embers at night to keep the fire alight.
14 Adjustable pot hanger.
15 Flesh hook for removing meat from a cauldron.
16 Iron knife.
17 If packed carefully, a cauldron could be used to cook many different things at once.
18 Three-legged cauldron for standing over the fire.
19 Narrow-necked iron cauldron for hanging above the fire.
20 Iron shears.
21 Thimble made from an alloy of copper.

On the farm

22 Mill stones. The grains of corn were ground into flour between the two stones.
23 Watermills had been known and used occasionally in Roman times, but because of the plentiful supply of slave labour there was little need to exploit them. However, from the 9th century they became much more common. The Domesday survey records 5,624 in England, about one to every fifty households.
24 Diagrammatic view of a water-driven flour-mill.
25 Fish trap. Poaching the lord's fish and game was a popular way of supplementing the family's diet.
26 Plunge churn for making butter.
27 Milking.
28 Wicker shoulder basket for carrying loads.
29-30 Copper alloy horse pendant and buckle from a leather bridle.
31 The clothes worn by a shepherd in medieval times.
32 Bed of coiled rope of straw used by peasants.
33 Peasant weeding with the implements of the time, a forked stick and curved blade.
34 Hand-operated rotary quern for grinding corn into flour. The stick fixed into the upper stone was turned by the miller, and the flour from the corn trickled into the sack held open below.

Farm tools

35 Iron-shod spade with different types of handle.
36 Sickle and bill-hooks.
37 Axes used by carpenters.
38 Tools for hay-making: scythe, rake and pitchfork.
39 Auger.

Ploughing

40 Reconstruction of the heavy plough common in medieval times.
41 Coulter which was used to open the ground in front of the ploughshare, so making ploughing easier and more effective.
42-43 Two versions of the heavy plough as shown in medieval manuscripts.
44 The light plough without a coulter could only be used in very light soils.
45 Light plough with coulter.
46 Ox-team drawing the heavy plough which could be used on heavy ground, so increasing the area of potential farmland.

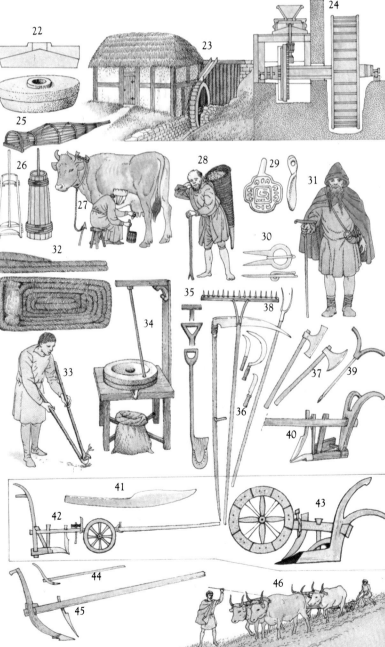

Monastic life

The monasteries of medieval Europe provided a distinctive way of life for many thousands of people. The earliest Christian monks were solitary hermits. The concept of a communal religious life, in which the individual was lost in the corporate worship of God, was the ideal of Benedict of Nursia who founded the Benedictine order in southern Italy in the 6th century.

A strictly ordered way of life

The regulations of the order were set out in the Rule of Benedict, and they were very strict. A timetable laid down the hours of prayer, work, meals and sleep. Prayers, the central point of a monk's existence, were to be performed seven times a day. The Roman day lasted from sunrise to sunset, and was divided into 12 equal hours whose length varied with the seasons. The monks therefore spent the same hours on their activities throughout the year, but not the same amount of time.

A water clock, regulated by a sundial, marked the passage of the hours by the flow of water from a graduated vessel. Mechanical clocks were invented in the late 13th century, but were not common until the 14th.

Monastic orders
1 Cistercian monk.
2 Franciscan friar.
3 Carthusian monk.
4 Dominican friar.

5 A pilgrim. Monasteries had to give hospitality to pilgrims.
6 Leper carrying a rattle to warn people of his approach.
7 Altar cross of gilt bronze. Putting a cross on the altar during mass seems to have started in the 13th century.
8 Benedictine sacristan. He cared for the sacred vessels.
9 Enamel pyx shaped like a dove.
10 Enamel candlestick.
11 Reliquary casket to hold the relics of a saint.
12 Patten for the consecrated host.
13 Chalice for the wine at mass.
14 Incense holder.
15 Monk checking an astrolabe.
16 Working on a manuscript.
17 Medieval illumination.
18 Writing desk which was put on the knee.
19 Abbot's ivory crozier.
20 Abbot giving the 'tonsure' to a new monk.
21 13th-century tonsure plate.
22 Hand warmer which contained hot charcoal.

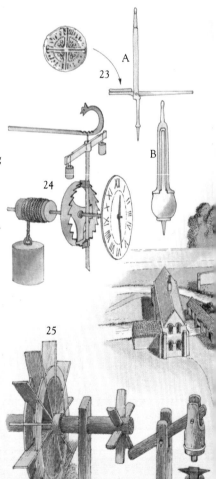

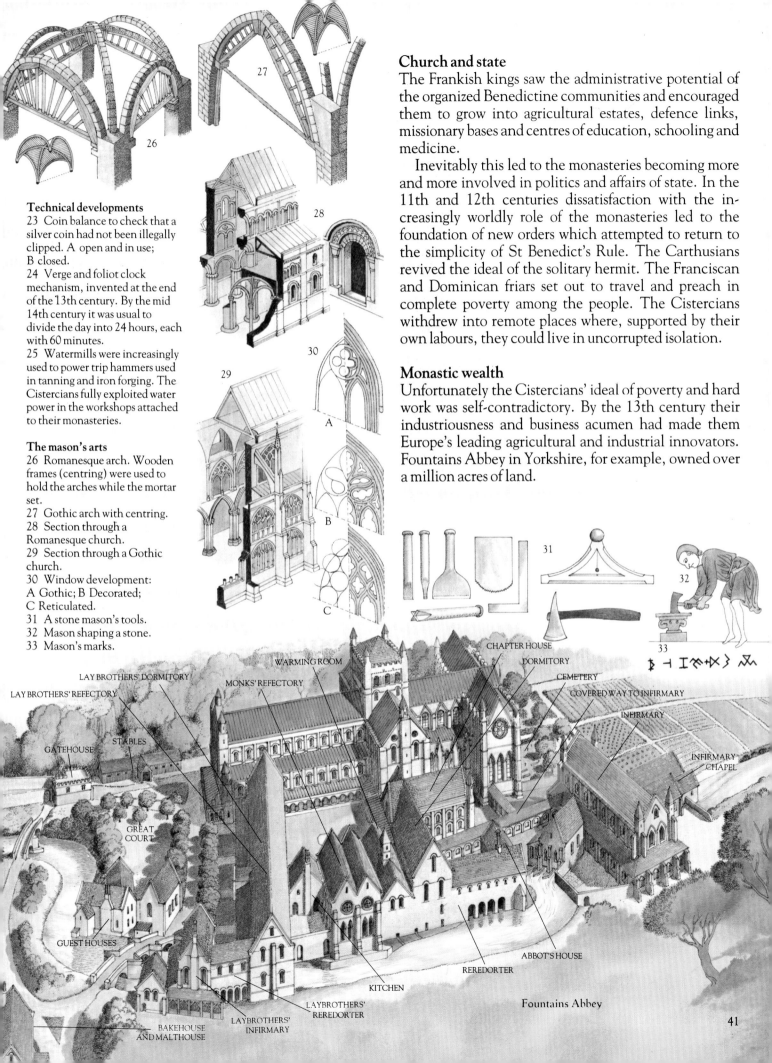

Technical developments

23 Coin balance to check that a silver coin had not been illegally clipped. A open and in use; B closed.

24 Verge and foliot clock mechanism, invented at the end of the 13th century. By the mid 14th century it was usual to divide the day into 24 hours, each with 60 minutes.

25 Watermills were increasingly used to power trip hammers used in tanning and iron forging. The Cistercians fully exploited water power in the workshops attached to their monasteries.

The mason's arts

26 Romanesque arch. Wooden frames (centring) were used to hold the arches while the mortar set.

27 Gothic arch with centring.

28 Section through a Romanesque church.

29 Section through a Gothic church.

30 Window development: A Gothic; B Decorated; C Reticulated.

31 A stone mason's tools.

32 Mason shaping a stone.

33 Mason's marks.

Church and state

The Frankish kings saw the administrative potential of the organized Benedictine communities and encouraged them to grow into agricultural estates, defence links, missionary bases and centres of education, schooling and medicine.

Inevitably this led to the monasteries becoming more and more involved in politics and affairs of state. In the 11th and 12th centuries dissatisfaction with the increasingly worldly role of the monasteries led to the foundation of new orders which attempted to return to the simplicity of St Benedict's Rule. The Carthusians revived the ideal of the solitary hermit. The Franciscan and Dominican friars set out to travel and preach in complete poverty among the people. The Cistercians withdrew into remote places where, supported by their own labours, they could live in uncorrupted isolation.

Monastic wealth

Unfortunately the Cistercians' ideal of poverty and hard work was self-contradictory. By the 13th century their industriousness and business acumen had made them Europe's leading agricultural and industrial innovators. Fountains Abbey in Yorkshire, for example, owned over a million acres of land.

Fountains Abbey

Tiling

6 Floor tiles inlaid with white pipe clay. The process originated on the Continent and reached England around 1200.

7 Reconstruction of a tile kiln found on a monastic grange. The arches which supported the tiles to be fired were made of removable fire bars (A). The kiln was covered with earth and turf through which the smoke from the fires (B) could percolate.

8 The wheelbarrow was in use in Europe around 1200, nearly 1000 years after its invention by the Chinese.

9 Pewter trading token used instead of money.

10 Blacksmith at work.

11 A Knight Templar.

12 Leather girdle with an alms bag attached.

13 Pottery chimney louvre. Roof ornaments like this became increasingly popular in the late 13th century.

Making cloth

1 Combing wool to align the long fibres before it is spun into thread.

2 The horizontal loom appeared in Europe in the 13th century.

3 Woman spinning with a distaff. Her hair is padded and netted in late 13th-century style.

4 Winter and summer dress. The winter overgarment has slits in the sleeves through which to put the arms.

5 13th-century gold brooch.

Windmills

14 A post-mill. The first windmills were built in the late 12th century and had become common by the 13th century. The body of the mill revolved on an oak post so that the sails could be brought round into the wind whatever direction it was blowing from. This seems to have been a European invention. Fixed windmills are known to have been used from the 7th century on the plateaux of Iran and Afghanistan, but the wind there only blew in one direction. Later the post-mill was refined so that only the sails had to be moved into the wind, not the entire body of the mill.

COWSHEDS · GRAIN STORE · MAIN ENTRANCE · GUARD ROOM · GUEST HOUSE · PIGSTIES · MILL POND · WATER MILL · FRUIT AND GENERAL STORE BARN · STABLES · HALL · WORKSHOP · HALL KEEP · KITCHEN · FISH POND · CHAPEL · IMPLEMENT AND WAGGON BARN

Knights Templars' estate

Reconstruction from archaeological evidence of the Knights Templars' estate at South Witham in Lincolnshire.

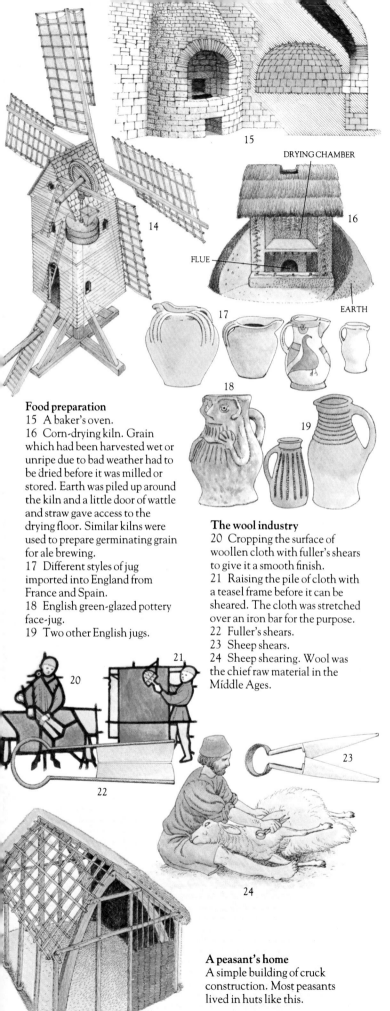

Food preparation

15 A baker's oven.

16 Corn-drying kiln. Grain which had been harvested wet or unripe due to bad weather had to be dried before it was milled or stored. Earth was piled up around the kiln and a little door of wattle and straw gave access to the drying floor. Similar kilns were used to prepare germinating grain for ale brewing.

17 Different styles of jug imported into England from France and Spain.

18 English green-glazed pottery face-jug.

19 Two other English jugs.

The wool industry

20 Cropping the surface of woollen cloth with fuller's shears to give it a smooth finish.

21 Raising the pile of cloth with a teasel frame before it can be sheared. The cloth was stretched over an iron bar for the purpose.

22 Fuller's shears.

23 Sheep shears.

24 Sheep shearing. Wool was the chief raw material in the Middle Ages.

A peasant's home
A simple building of cruck construction. Most peasants lived in huts like this.

Monasteries and agriculture

The Cistercians were not the only monastic order which farmed. All monasteries tried to be as self-sufficient as possible, and so became involved in farming to a greater or lesser extent. The Cistercians, however, were more successful than many other orders. This is shown in the fine buildings they put up, for example at Fountains (see page 41).

Many religious orders were given land by pious people, who hoped to find favour both in this world and the next. This helped increase the estates and so the wealth of the monastic orders. As they consolidated these holdings, by buying more land, they turned them into highly organized model farms or 'granges'. These played an important part in the reclamation of thousands of acres of wasteland throughout Europe, by clearing woods, draining marshes, and irrigating dry, uncultivable heathland.

The Templars – warriors and farmers

The Templars were an order of knights formed after the First Crusade (1096-9) to guard the routes to the Holy Land and protect the holy places. Until their dissolution in 1308 they held large estates very similar to those of the Cistercians. Remains of one dating from the 13th century have been excavated at South Witham, Lincolnshire.

As reconstructed by the archaeologists, the Templar estate had a good range of buildings, although of a simpler and less grandiose design than those built on granges belonging to the Cistercians. The domestic accommodation included a single-storey hall with a central hearth and a roof span of 10m., which shows that the builders knew of the most recent roofing techniques. At the west end of the hall was a solar, the private quarters of the resident Templar or the bailiff.

The chapel was built in a quiet inner court. Inside, the chapel was divided by a wall into a section for the Templars on the east, and for the laity and farmworkers on the west.

The kitchen compound also contained workshops. From excavations we know that there were furnaces for lead and iron smelting, a tile kiln and a corn-drying kiln. A considerable staff would have been needed for all these activities. Similar Cistercian granges had up to 20 servants, in addition to the lay brethren who supervised them.

So successful were the monastic agriculturalists that by the 13th century a very large part of the arable farmland of Europe belonged to them, and almost every lay landowner would have had a member of a religious order as his neighbour.

A medieval town

When country people had a surplus of eggs, corn or vegetables to sell, they needed a good trading place, no further away than they could walk in a day, with time to sell their wares and get home again before dark. Medieval towns grew up to serve this need. They were market centres which flourished at some focal point: where roads crossed, where there was a harbour or an important bridge, or in the protective shelter of a castle or monastery.

Many medieval towns were little more than large villages by today's standards, even the more important ones. By the beginning of the 15th century, for example, it is estimated that there were still only five towns in England, London, York, Bristol, Coventry and Norwich, which had more than 2,000 houses.

A medieval town house

The house shown opposite probably belonged to a fairly prosperous family. Known today as 'The Hall', Ivy Lane, it was built in Canterbury at the end of the 14th century, and is typical of its period.

The Hall, and all other medieval timber buildings that still stand, owe their survival to the fact that their walls rest on footings of stone. This advance in building technique was first used in the 11th century. Before this wooden buildings were supported by their posts which were set fairly deeply into the ground, but this meant that the building only lasted until the posts rotted. The new system created a rigid self-supporting structure. This, in turn, enabled more skilful methods of carpentry to develop, and more elaborate decoration on houses became worthwhile.

Houses like the Hall had developed from the Saxon aisled hall, and existed largely unchanged from the 13th to the 15th centuries. As long as houses had central open fires, as they had to in the days before stone chimneys, they could not have a complete upper storey. Upper chambers, however, were made at the gable ends to provide a private room for the owner of the house. Underneath was often a parlour or storeroom. At the other end of the house was a buttery and pantry with the servants' quarters above.

Two doors opposite each other in the long walls provided a front entrance for the family and important visitors, and a back door leading to the stables and kitchen buildings – a very draughty arrangement before the introduction of protective screens.

Household goods
1 Socketed candlestick.
2 Bed frame.
3 Metal key.
4 Lantern of copper alloy, its window shielded by horn or glass.
5 Bronze pricket candlestick with folding legs. The round socket may have been for a rushlight.
6 Green glazed pottery jugs.
7 Ram's head jug.
8 Three-legged jug.
9 Bronze skillet.
10 Three-legged bronze ewer.

▷ **The kitchen**
Because of the risk of fire in timber buildings, it was usual in medieval times for the kitchen to be a separate building behind the house. If there was an oven it was sometimes in a separate bakehouse, or built on to the back of the house.

▽ **The façade** of the house opposite, showing the fall-front counter of the shop.

FRONT DOOR

SHOP WINDOW

COUNTER

STONE FOOTINGS

Carpentry

11 Sawing planks with a frame saw. This superseded the earlier type.

12 How to cut a tree trunk to get the maximum number of planks.

13 Carpenter's tools: A brace; B mallet; C chisel; D bow saw; E siding-up axes for trimming beams; F auger for boring holes.

14 Long saw for cutting beams.

15 Using a plane. The plane was known in antiquity, and Roman ones were almost identical to those used today.

Building methods

16 Roof support. The weight was taken by a central post, the crown post, which rested on a tie beam which spanned the building. The house below had 3 crown posts.

17 Scarf joint used inside walls.

18-23 Roof constructions used in larger buildings from the mid-13th century: 18 tickeredge and truss; 19 hammer-beam; 20 base cruck; 21 tie beam; 22 boarhunt end truss; 23 boarhunt and base cruck truss.

△ The Hall in Ivy Lane, Canterbury

The central ground floor hall rises to the full height of the roof, but the upper chambers at each end jut out over the street.

In the buttery on the left are casks of wine and ale; a meal chest for flour or grain stands on the floor. Above is the bedroom of the owner and his wife.

The earth floors were swept and covered with fresh rushes. A chess board hangs on the wall. Beside the spinning wheel is the winder for the thread.

To the right is the shop – a general store selling purses, belts and kitchen ware. The customer stood in the street and was served through the window.

Markets and trading

No town could hold a market without permission from the king, although sometimes he gave this right to a feudal lord in return for a large fee. Because of the profits to be made from renting out shops and stalls and from tolls levied on the goods that outsiders brought in to sell, towns were eager to pay the king for the right to hold a market. If a king was short of money, granting this right was a quick and painless source of revenue: there were 3,000 such grants in England in the 13th century alone.

Control of trade

Different foods had to be sold in specific areas of the town or market so that their quality could be easily inspected. Bakers were often in court for selling poor quality or undersized loaves. Anyone who sold bad wine could be forced to drink it in public.

The running of the market was in the hands of the merchant guild which, in the early days, was made up of any town traders who had paid an entrance fee and sworn an oath of loyalty. They elected the guild officers of whom the chief was the 'alderman'. These officials were often the same influential men chosen to form the town corporation, though the chief citizen was known by the Norman name of 'Mayor'.

Town craftsmen

The trading opportunities towns offered attracted all kinds of different craftsmen. The newly created borough of Stratford-upon-Avon in the 13th century had fullers, dyers, tanners, shoemakers, tailors, glovemakers, carpenters, tilers, coopers, locksmiths, oilmakers, ropemakers and wheel-wrights.

Craftsmen usually lived on the premises where they worked, and sold their goods through an unglazed window at the front of the house. Men of the same trade congregated in the same part of town. These formed specialized local markets which have given their names to streets such as Goldsmiths' Row and Ironmonger Row.

Craft guilds

Craft guilds grew out of these trading communities. Originally religious associations for mutual aid and charity, they became trade societies which laid down strict regulations for each craft. These governed trading standards, terms of apprenticeship and admission as a master craftsman. Any member breaching the rules could be severely punished. No-one who was not a member of a guild could practise its craft.

Town costume
1 A merchant of the mid-14th century. He wears a coif on his head, a tunic and cloak.
2 Woman's dress with long decorative sleeves.
3 Young girl wearing a cote-hardie with the sides cut away to show the undergarment.
4 Silver ring brooch.
5 Copper alloy belt buckles.
6 Leather boot.
7 Belt catch, 1390.

8 Ivory mirror back. The circular mirror of which this was the case was of polished steel.
9 Bone comb.
10 Spectacles. These were invented in Italy in the 1290s, although simple lenses had been known for centuries. The earliest spectacles folded shut.
11 14th-century buttons. The tight cloths of the period were fastened with long rows of buttons.
12 Scissors, 14th century.
13 Shears with engraved blades.

Living in town

14 An indenture. An agreement between two people was written twice on a sheet of parchment or paper. It was then cut in two along a zigzag (indented) line. Each party kept half. In any dispute the two pieces could be matched. An indenture was also an agreement between master and apprentice.

15 Seal and impression.

16 Bone stylus for writing on a wax tablet.

17 Lead stylus, the medieval pencil, used for ruling parchment or paper.

18 Letters of the 14th century Lombardic alphabet: A, L, F, H, M, T, U, L, E.

19 Groat or 4-penny piece, 1351.

20 Embossed leather book cover.

21 Steel gauntlet from armour.

22 Leather water bottle.

23 Sword with inscribed blade.

24 Kidney dagger.

25 Leather knife sheath.

26 14th-century helmet with chain mail to protect the throat.

27 Horse pendant.

28 Badge worn by a pilgrim who had been to Canterbury.

29 Lead plague cross.

30 Reliquary: A, open; B, closed.

31 Pilgrim's souvenir.

32 Silver spoon; A handle detail.

33 Spinning wheel. Yarn could be spun with a clockwise (B) or anti-clockwise (A) twist. Carding implements (C) were used to prepare fibres for spinning.

34 Water seller with skin water containers.

35 Well bucket.

36 Messenger, probably working for a rich man whose emblem is shown on his message box (A).

37 Cross section of an inn. The ground plan (B) shows the large number of shops crammed into it.

▽**Medieval people**

A throng of people, such as would have been seen in any typical town street in the mid-14th century.

A Knight with his squire; it was thought beneath the dignity of a knight to travel alone.

B Widow wearing the 'barbe' or mourning headdress.

C Franciscan friar.

D Woman wearing a surcoat. Her hand is in a slit in it which allowed her to reach the purse hanging at her waist from a belt under the surcoat.

E Two Italian merchants.

F Tinker carrying a pack with his tools.

G Bailiff in town for his lord.

H Peasant woman and child.

A brief chronology

753 BC Rome founded. Celtic tribes settle in Britain (c. 600 BC). 509 BC Rome becomes republic. 146 BC Roman power in Mediterranean consolidated by defeat of Carthage. Rome extends sovereignty over neighbouring countries. 55 and 54 BC Julius Caesar's first expeditions to Britain. Conquest of Gaul.

50 BC A CELTIC FARMER (page 4)

44 BC Assassination of Julius Caesar. Augustus becomes Emperor. Roman civilization at its peak. Empire expanded. Birth of Christ.

AD 15 A ROMAN VILLA (page 8)

AD 43 Britain conquered. London founded. Roman provinces mostly peaceful but riots in Rome. Emperors increasingly corrupt. Civil war and disorder until Vespasian restores peace in AD 69.

100 ROMAN TOWN LIFE (page 12)

Hadrian's Wall built (c. 122) to mark and defend northern limit of empire. Christianity begins to make converts and spread through empire.

150 VINDOLANDA: THE FRONTIER (page 16)

Attacks by northern tribes continue and intensify. 292 Diocletian divides empire into two. Persecution of Christians. 330 Constantine founds Constantinople as empire's new capital. Christianity becomes official religion. Empire under severe pressure from barbarian attacks. 410 Roman troops leave Britain. Barbarians flood into Europe. 449 Saxons begin all-out conquest of Britain. 455 Rome sacked by Vandals. 486 Clovis, king of Franks, becomes Christian.

500 THE ANGLO-SAXON INVADERS (page 20)

Anglo Saxon settlement of eastern Britain. 529 Benedictine Order founded. Papal authority grows. 570 Birth of Mohammed and rise of Muslim faith. 597 Christian missionaries land in Britain. Constantinople becomes a powerful sea-state.

700 BYZANTIUM: THE NEW ROME (page 24)

Moslems (Moors) conquer Egypt and whole of N. Africa, attack Constantinople, occupy Spain. Spread of Christianity. Moors held back in northern Spain. 800 Charlemagne becomes Holy Roman Emperor. First attacks by Northmen (Vikings) in N. Europe.

800 THE ARABS IN EUROPE (page 28)

Norse attacks increase; settle in Ireland, Scotland, penetrate Russia, Mediterranean, settle in Normandy. Continuous raids against England. Christianity spreads to Scandinavia and E. Europe. Byzantine Empire remains strong. Learning flourishes in Italy.

1000 THE VIKINGS, MASTERS OF THE SEA (page 32)

1066 Norman conquest of England. Moors in Spain pushed back by El Cid (1040-99). 1086 Domesday Book compiled. Seljuk Turks attack Constantinople, capture Jerusalem. 1095 Urban II preaches First Crusade. 1099 Jerusalem captured by Crusaders.

1100 CASTLE AND MANOR HOUSE (page 36)

1135-54 Civil war in England. 1170 Murder of Thomas à Becket. 1187 Saladin captures Jerusalem. Third Crusade under Richard I. Constantinople most cultured city in Europe. Rise of N. German trading cities. Universities founded at Oxford, Paris.

1200 MONASTIC LIFE (page 40)

1215 Magna Carta signed. Fourth Crusade and sack of Constantinople. Mongols invade Poland, Hungary. Frederick III unites Spain, repulses Moors. War between England and Scotland ends. Crusaders retire to Cyprus. 1290 Jews expelled from England.

1300 A MEDIEVAL TOWN (page 44)

Hanseatic League founded, with trading monopoly. Growth of strong merchant class. Outbreak of Hundred Years' War (1337-1453). 1348 Black Death reduces population by a third. Introduction of Gothic Perpendicular style of architecture. Prosperity and culture of Italian city states; Medicis rule Florence. House of Hapsburg supreme in C. Europe. 1431 Joan of Arc burned at stake. English routed from France. 1453 Fall of Constantinople; end of Byzantine empire.

Booklist

With a subject as wide-ranging as this, there are many hundreds of excellent books in which to continue research. Here are some that you might find helpful:

A CELTIC FARMER *Farming in the Iron Age* by P.J. Reynolds (Cambridge University Press, 1977); *The Celts* by T.G.E. Powell (Thames & Hudson, 1974).

A ROMAN VILLA *Country Life in Classical Times* by D.K. White (Paul Elek, 1977); *Roman Farming* by D.K. White (Thames & Hudson, 1970).

ROMAN TOWN LIFE *Pompeii* by P. Connolly (Macdonald Educational, 1979); *Roman Society* by D. Dudley (Penguin, 1975).

VINDOLANDA *Vindolanda: a Roman frontier post on Hadrian's Wall* by R. Birley (Thames & Hudson, 1979); *The Roman Army* by P. Connolly (Macdonald Educational, 1975).

THE ANGLO-SAXONS *The Archaeology of Anglo-Saxon England* ed. by D.M. Wilson (Methuen, 1977); *The Anglo-Saxons, How They Lived and Worked* by G.A. Lester (David & Charles, 1976).

BYZANTIUM *Byzantium* by P. Sherrard (Time-Life International, 1977); *The Byzantines* by D. Talbot-Rice (Thames & Hudson, 1975).

THE ARABS IN EUROPE *Muslim Spain* by D. Townson (Cambridge University Press, 1979); *Islamic Art* by D. Talbot-Rice (Thames & Hudson, 1979).

THE VIKINGS *The Viking World* by J. Graham Campbell (Frances Lincoln, 1980); *The Vikings and their origins* by D.M. Wilson (Thames & Hudson, 1979).

CASTLE AND MANOR HOUSE *English Medieval Castles* by R.A. Brown (Batsford, 1976); *Life on the English Manor* by H.S. Bennett (Cambridge University Press, 1974).

MONASTIC LIFE *English Abbeys* by H. Braun (Faber, 1971); *The Medieval Machine* by J. Gimpel (Gollancz, 1977).

A MEDIEVAL TOWN *Medieval Craftsmen* by J. Harvey (Batsford, 1975); *The English Medieval Town* by C. Platt (Paladin, 1979).